peaceful spaces

alice whately

peaceful spaces

transform your home into a haven of calm and tranquillity

RYLAND
PETERS
& SMALL

LONDON NEW YORK

For Barty, with all my love

First published in the USA in 2002
by Ryland Peters & Small, Inc.
519 Broadway, 5th Floor
New York, NY 10012
www.rylandpeters.com

10 9 8 7 6 5 4 3 2 1

Design, text and photographs
© Ryland Peters & Small 2002

ISBN 1 84172 263 4

Library of Congress Cataloging-in-Publication Data is available
on request

Printed and bound in China

Picture credits
Front Jacket: photographer David Montgomery/Belinda
and Guy Battle's house, designed by Mathew Priestman

Senior designer Sally Powell

Senior editor Sophie Bevan

Location and picture research manager Kate Brunt

Picture researchers Jenny Drane and Emily Westlake

Production Deborah Wehner

Art director Gabriella Le Grazie

Publishing director Alison Starling

CONTENTS

Since ancient times, the home has provided a sense of belonging, affection, and togetherness around which we are able to structure our lives. Today, this concept is more important than ever as the frenetic pace of modern living increases our desire to retreat to a soothing haven where we can nurture mind, body, and soul.

INTRODUCTION

To focus on underlying fundamentals so they can give more

As a result, the creation of a peaceful environment is at the forefront of contemporary design requirements. Taking its inspiration from the dictates of Zen minimalism, this soothing style combines spontaneous simplicity with natural materials in order to create an effective antidote to the stresses and strains of life in the 21st century.

Other-worldly though it may sound, there is no great mystery to the creation of the "soul home." Instead, it is a simple case of paring down your interior in order to allow the intrinsic beauty of light, texture, and shape to form the decoration. Neither is the concept of a spiritual environment confined to the bedroom or living area. Instead, this design directive is an holistic one—as applicable in the home office as it is in the bathroom—enabling you to create the sort of serene retreat you thought was the exclusive domain of the luxury health spa.

PART ONE

the theory

"Space and light and order. These are the things men need just as much as they need bread or a place to sleep."

Le Corbusier (1887–1965)

Clean lines, simple colors and lots of natural light are the main components of the successful spiritual space (below and opposite). By creating living areas with these specifications in mind, the thoughts of the rooms' inhabitants are able to roam free from the constraints of the outside world.

space clearing

By questioning the purpose of everything you own, you will quickly realize that it is you, rather than the stuff that surrounds you, that must take center stage in the home.

Commonly viewed as a Japanese concept, Zen philosophy actually originated in China, where monks merged Indian Buddhism and Chinese Taoism in a bid to find the true path to spiritual enlightenment. In 1190, Zen Buddhism was enthusiastically adopted by the Japanese, who developed the idea that simplicity was synonymous with spirituality and applied it to every aspect of their lives—including their homes.

The sense of harmony found in Zen's design style transmits similar feelings of serenity to its occupants— and has been reinterpreted by Western designers and architects since the nineteenth century. Today, the Zen interior has become a refuge from the outside world where busy roads, new technology, and the cult of consumerism leaves us feeling anxious and unfulfilled.

As a result, more and more of us are turning to the ancient philosophies of the East in order to regain a sense of spirituality in our domestic lives. Increasingly, our homes are becoming places of sanctuary where simple Zen aesthetics help to calm the senses, inspire creativity, and induce clarity of thought.

help to support you and so supports these things about you.

CREATING A BLANK CANVAS

In order to turn your home into a haven of peace and tranquillity, you must first look closely at the availability of space and light. To do this, walk slowly through each room; scrutinize the floors, walls, and windows, and consider the following options. Are there any walls you could knock down or replace with loadbearing pillars? Is it possible to insert more windows or to raise the height of existing ones? Could your install a skylight? Does your carpet cover space-enhancing boards or antique parquet?

Next, look at your furniture and fixtures and ask yourself what you could do without. If you're scrupulously honest, you may well discover that many things you thought were indispensable to domestic bliss are, in fact, easily dispensed with.

The theory of space clearing combines the physical process of removing unnecessary clutter with the aesthetic one of simplifying your surroundings. For example, if you use the same color for your walls and floors, your home will immediately feel calmer and more cohesive. Similarly, if you employ flexible devices, such as sliding doors, pull-out shelves, fold-up tables, and wheeled units, your space will instantly appear sleeker and more streamlined.

It is also important to think laterally. Necessary white goods don't have to fit into their allocated rooms just because tradition demands it. For example, if you have a tiny kitchen, plumb your washing machine into a bathroom cabinet, or keep your tumble dryer in a cupboard under the stairs if you're pushed for space elsewhere.

When it comes to making decisions about your home, it's important to listen to your instincts. This way you will reconnect with your spiritual self—and create an environment that nurtures your heart and soul. By stripping your home of the things that fail to inspire you, you make space for the things that do.

A single color scheme in a living area (opposite) enables the jutting angles of the fireplace, sloping roof, and beamed ceiling to combine seamlessly for a coherent whole. A white-on-white room also makes your space look bigger, allowing for the addition of a large sofa, comfortable chairs, and a smattering of gently curved objects, which soften the look.

Again, white effectively opens up a space, giving a narrow corridor through the kitchen (above) a feeling of lightness and expansiveness. The overall look is much more workaday than the floaty feel of the living room next door, thanks to a scrubbed wooden table and worktop. In addition, darkly colored ornaments help anchor the look.

If you love books, for instance, celebrate your literary leanings by building a huge bookcase. Similarly, if music soothes your soul, install a huge sofa and allow yourself to listen in comfort and peace.

CLUTTER CRUSHES THE SPIRIT

The philosophy of clearing your space and hence your mind is one that works for most people. According to Zen principles, clutter is an accumulation of anything that impedes the vital flow of "chi"— or essential energy—in the home. Without the presence of chi, it is impossible to turn your living environment into a place where your thoughts and actions are spirited and spontaneous.

In order to attain a clutter-free space, you must first prune your possessions with the religious zeal of one determined to see the light.

What could be a dingy staircase is actually an attractive feature (above)**, thanks to the combination of pale scrubbed wood and white-painted walls. The knots and gnarls in the wood add extra interest, as do the colorful masks sitting on the landing shelf.**

Does your response to a thing take away from you?
Are there so many things that the accumulated give & take affects generate an overall response that takes energy away from you?

The elegant lines of an art-school drawing chest (left) **provide excellent storage space. Here, the calming symmetry of the slim drawers is balanced by a handful of natural ornaments—an unframed canvas, an air-purifying orchid, woodcarvings, and fossil fragments—to produce a look that is as calm as it is aesthetic.**

Not only do the floaty drapes offer a feeling of softness to the minimalist bedroom (opposite)**, but they also help to diffuse harsh light, creating an ambient feeling of tranquillity.**

15

The heavy appearance of a dark wooden tallboy (far left) is given a fresh and contemporary feel through the addition of a pair of wicker baskets. The soft curves of the chair and light tones of the natural floor covering also help lift the look.

A skylight (left) is an ideal way make sure your space is filled with natural light. The flood of sunlight also provides a connection to the natural world which, together with the introduction of greenery, is essential for attaining a feeling of spiritual vitality within the home.

Anything you no longer use, want, or like should either be thrown away or given to a charity. This includes shoes, clothes, and kitchenware, as well as CDs you no longer listen to, photographs that will never make it into the album, and books you're unlikely to read. It is also important to rid your home of negative energy, which is manifested through plants that are dead or dying and anything that has been broken for a long time or has parts missing.

THE POWER OF WHITE
Think of any peaceful space designed to nurture the spirit—be it a yoga studio, a chapel, a spiritual retreat, or an holistic spa—and you can be sure its walls will be painted a light, bright shade of white. The color of purity, cleanliness, and peace, white is key to creating a spiritual environment, offering a sense of luminosity that acts as an effective salve for the soul.

White also contains all colors. 17

The advantages of living in a serene white cube are numerous. Not only do walls painted in pale shades reflect natural light, making your space seem bigger and brighter, but the continuity of color also helps to prevent fragmentation. The bluish tint of ultra-white, however, can seem cold and stark unless you live in a sunny place. Instead, opt for creamier tones, which will turn your home into a sanctuary of softness and warmth.

An all-white color scheme also allows for a multitude of textural contrasts. For example, juxtapose untreated concrete walls with a shiny lacquered floor to create a shell of subtle contradictions, or pair a white wicker chair with a pristine silk cushion for

continuity of color prevents fragmentation

a look that is interestingly discreet rather than bland and boring. Sticking to a pale palette also allows for the creation of instantly dramatic focal points through the occasional bolt of brilliant color. For instance, contrast a vase of orange gerberas or a jewel-bright rug against a blank canvas and—presto—your decoration is complete.

SALVATION THROUGH STORAGE
However diligently you clear your clutter, you will still need storage space for functional items such as linen, blankets, tools, cleaning products, stationery and paperwork, which all need to be stowed away. It is also important to remember that you will need more storage than you think. Collections of books, CDs, ceramics, and shoes never get smaller, only larger, and situations change (you may want to start a family, a new hobby, a fitness regime—all of which demand additional space).

A white and cream color scheme (above) illustrates the strong impact of pared-down decoration. The flimsy cotton shade allows for lots of natural illumination, while a pebble and the antiquated pitcher filled with a simple bunch of daisies, create an aesthetic focal point.

Textural contrast is vital in the all-white room (right), where the roughly painted wood table and bumpy wicker chairs are juxtaposed with the sheer fabric of the curtains and smooth surface of the milk bottle, glasses, and shiny plates.

Clearing clutter in the workspace is essential for creating an atmosphere that is conducive to concentration (this page). Here, a selection of box files, plus a couple of sets of small filing drawers, keep things in their place without appearing overly regimented. The desktop is kept clear, save for vital pieces of equipment.

A selection of attractive spiral-bound notebooks and a pretty floral paperweight (left) help to keep your thoughts—and paperwork—in order, and prove that organization in the peaceful workspace does not need to look dull and "officey" to be effective.

Not only are box files (below) a great way for filing office paperwork, but they can also be used for storing magazines. In this orderly office, a combination of labeled box files and storage boxes with lids is ranged along neat cubicle shelving, providing the user with quick and easy access to important documents and periodicals. The soft aqua color scheme is a calming departure from the more masculine colors often associated with office storage.

The good news about modern storage is its spiritually sympathetic design. Buy a built-in cabinet these days, and you get a beautifully streamlined piece of furniture that adds to, rather than detracts from, the cohesive look you want to achieve. Better still, most modern units come with pop-open door mechanisms or flush-fit handles, so your storage units can blend seamlessly with the room's overall decor.

Another option is to implement structural storage that fits into the framework of your space. This can be achieved by replacing partition walls with floor-to-ceiling units accessible from both sides. Modular compartments provide a mix of open-and-shut storage space, while recessed shelving gives a truly streamlined result.

Once you start exploring the potential for storage in your home, you will discover an abundance of "dead areas" begging to be exploited. For example, slot drawers or a large chest beneath the bed; install a pull-out laundry bin under the bathroom basin; or sidestep the need for a dressing table by creating a niche—complete with electric sockets—in a closet.

HEAVENLY CONTAINERS

The calming home has a cohesive appearance. It should be a place where your eyes and mind can roam free from the constraints of consumerism. To attain this purity of vision, it is essential that you keep vulgar packaging to a

Modern units need not be dull simply because they are functional; instead, make a feature of your storage solutions by choosing contemporary cubes (right) and stacking them in a seemingly spontaneous tower, supported by a central rod. In this way you will achieve excellent storage that is also attractive.

Structural storage that fits into the framework of your space (opposite) is a wonderful way to keep clutter hidden from view, while wall-to-wall storage units are ideal for streamlining your space. In addition, foldaway or multifunctional furniture will help keep your living areas as clear as possible.

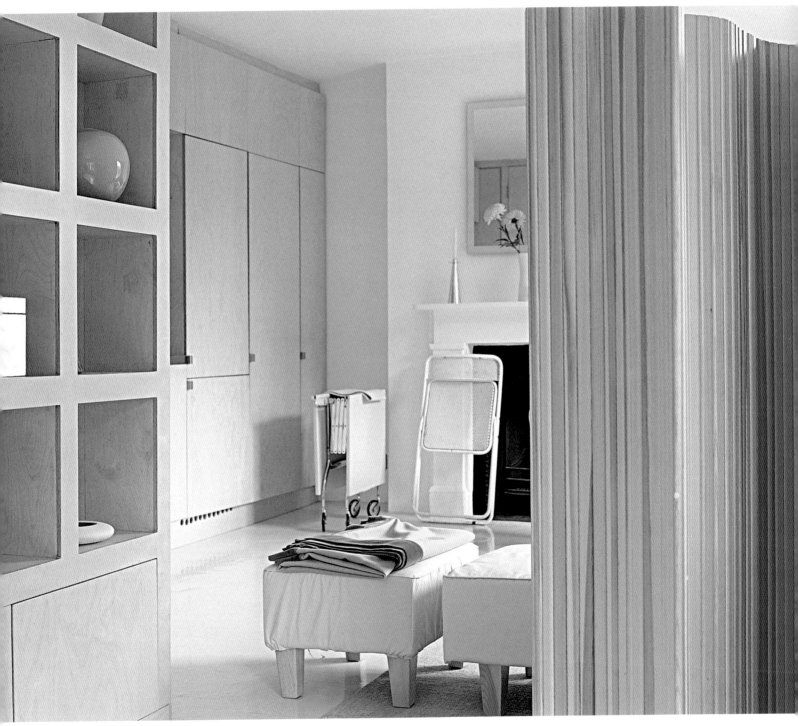

Natural light is an essential feature in the creation of a peaceful living environment (right and opposite), helping to generate energy, amplify space, and nurture the soul. In addition, according to the philosophy of feng shui, a daily dose of fresh air is essential for ridding your home of stale yin energy. As a result, it is imperative that you harness as much light as possible, and it is worth considering the installation of more windows or increasing the size of existing ones in your home. Alternatively, you can also explore the possibilities of installing French doors, skylights, or a solarium.

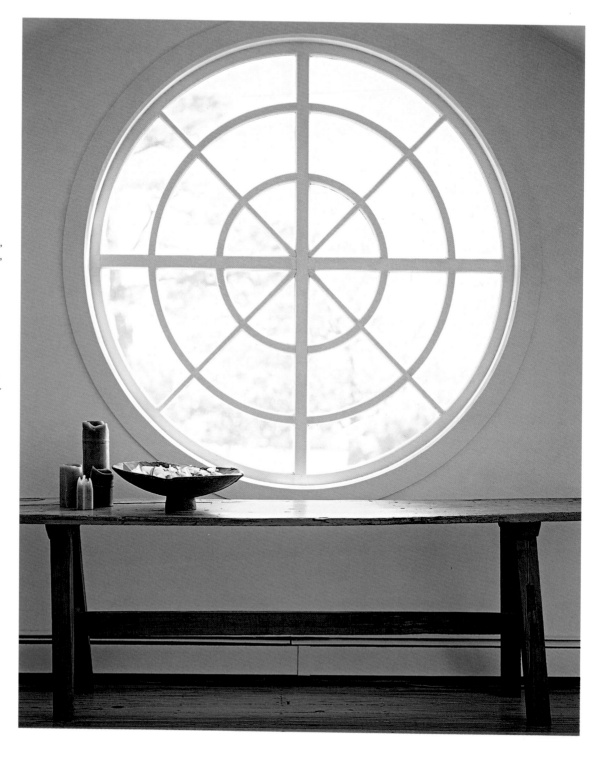

minimum (nothing jars like the lurid logo of a domestic cleaner). Decant everything you buy into attractive containers and your home will become an instantly—and blissfully—brand-free zone.

It doesn't matter what containers you choose to decant into, as long as you group similar ones together. For example, transfer dry goods such as pasta, flour, rice, and cereal into identical glass jars; put liquid detergent, cotton balls, and toothpaste into sisal or wicker pots, and fill ceramic bottles—complete with dispensing pumps—with shampoo, conditioner, moisturizer, and liquid soap.

SEEING THE LIGHT

Consider any soulful experience—biblical or otherwise—and you will find that it has a strong dependence on the purity of light. As a result, it is easy to see why light is a key factor in the creation of a home that will nurture the spirit: light helps to harness energy, to amplify space, and to generate feelings of optimism and goodwill.

The best illumination for your space and for your spirit is daylight, a natural phenomenon that should be exploited to the full. This means exploring the possibilities of installing more windows, increasing the size of existing ones, and introducing skylights. Alternatively, take the light-enhancing process a step farther and construct a solarium or conservatory.

It is also possible to maximize daylight by keeping windows as clean and clear as possible: if you have curtains, tie them back during the day or, better still, replace them with light-filtering blinds. In addition, keep the exterior of your windows clear by pruning vines and branches. Move light-blocking pieces of furniture to the other side of the room and make sure your windowsills are kept free of ornaments.

If you are unable to keep your windows completely clear—you may be overlooked by neighbors, for

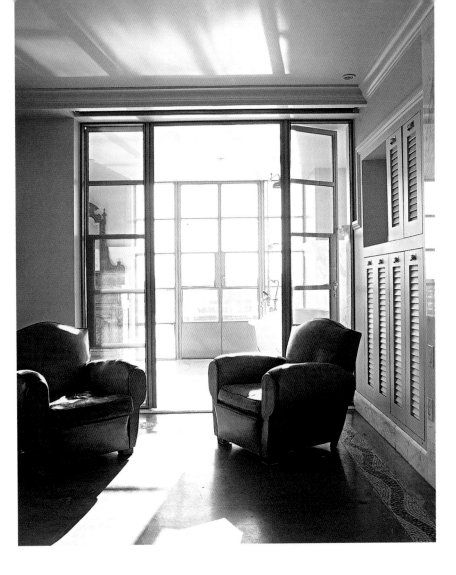

example—cover the bottom half of the windows with a translucent fabric, such as linen, cotton, or voile. Similarly, if the glare is too harsh, try venetian blinds, sandblasted glass, or tracing paper—all of which help diffuse light and create thought-provoking shadows.

In terms of artificial lighting, a strictly minimalist approach is advised: replace overhead lights with subtle uplighters; choose wall-mounted lights over table lamps to keep surfaces clear; and wire lights to circuits operated from a single panel to reduce the need for ugly sockets and trailing cords. You can extend the range of your lighting by putting in bulbs of varying wattage, controlled by individual circuits.

The beneficial impact of
color on our mood is well
documented by psychologists
around the world. Combine
color with light, however, and
the effect on the psyche is truly
remarkable. A bedroom painted
blue (this page) **creates a serene
sense of peace and tranquillity,
while the pretty diamond
patterns created by the
honeycomb glass ceiling**
(opposite) **are not only
aesthetically attractive, but also
help to promote feelings of
optimism and energy, thanks to
the shifting nature of the warm
patches of light.**

MOOD HUES

The concept of matching your lighting to your mood
is an immensely seductive one. Better still, thanks to
hip hoteliers Ian Schrager and Philippe Starck it is
now a realistic option in the home. Kicking off with
the Mondrian in Los Angeles, where colored light
installations funk up the hotel's clean white space, the
design duo have taken the concept a step farther at a
London hotel, St. Martin's Lane, which allows guests
to illuminate their clinical white rooms by dialing up
the color of their choice.

Even better, Colorwash, the lighting system used by
Schrager and Starck, is now available retail—allowing
homeowners to mood-light their interiors in subtle
tones that can be changed from blue to violet and
red to green at the flick of a switch.

27

By carefully choosing and positioning your furnishings, you will
discover the beauty in harmony and simplicity.

balance and form

To achieve harmony in the home, it is vital to create
a balance between form and function. This concept
derives from the Zen aesthetic of yin and yang or, in
layman's terms, opposing forces which, when equally
represented, create a harmonious balance of energy.

The energy in our homes is in a constant state of
flux, so achieving the perfect balance between yin
(cool, dark, and lifeless) and yang (hot, bright, and full
of life) is essential if we are to create a calming and
cosmic atmosphere. The best way to introduce both
yin and yang into the home is through the natural
elements of fire, water, earth, metal, and wood—the
fundamental types of energy found in all substances
and phenomena. When these elements are equally
represented, their synergy will create the vitally
spiritual environment we seek.

It is not necessary to introduce the five elements
into your home in their raw states, however. Instead,
each can be represented symbolically, or through color
or texture. For example, if you haven't enough space
for an indoor water feature, use an indigo pillow or
a turquoise vase in its place. Similarly, fire can be

The sinuous curves of a plain ceramic vase (top) cast a wonderful two-toned shadow, while the uncompromising lines of the lamp (above) are softened by the burnt-umber shade.

The forces of yin and yang are represented (right) through the use of color: the orange disks in the paintings signify fire; and the brown background, earth. Similarly, the turquoise pillow represents water, and the spray of blossom symbolizes wood.

In a perfect example of balance and form, the decorative objects surrounding the fireplace (this page) work on a number of different levels. The serene symmetry of the lacquered jars provides a smooth complement to the coarser fibers of the shallow basket placed in the grate, and their glossy sheen is echoed in the black frame of the picture propped up against the wall. Rigid lines contrast with soft curves to compound the effect, while the jars' off-center positioning creates a balanced whole.

A sure way to enhance energy in the home is to use contrasting colors (opposite). Here, the combination of sea blue with yellow kickstarts an otherwise somber room, effectively preventing the dark woods from dominating.

represented by a candle or an orange lantern; earth, by pebbles; wood, by house plants; and metal, by a silver photograph frame.

Spiritual energy is also wrought through the force of contradiction. The collision of new and old, hot and cold, and decorative and plain, all create an electrical current that runs between opposites. A good example of this is the energy charge created by the use of contrasting colors. This works particularly well with a predominantly neutral palette, where the juxtaposition of pink and yellow or brown and turquoise gives potentially bland spaces a life-enhancing jolt.

DECORATING WITH A SIXTH SENSE

Feng shui has been practiced for the past four thousand years and derives from the Chinese Taoist science for divining the healthy and prosperous layout of the home. This means decorating in order to harness *chi* (the vital life force) and avoid *sha* (noxious vapors).

If the energy in your home becomes blocked—or allowed to flow too swiftly—it can cause corresponding blockages and problems in life. Luckily, misspent energy is easily corrected. At its core, feng shui teaches that, by making small shifts in the arrangement of

According to the philosophy of feng shui, large mirrors are an excellent way to generate positive yang energy in a living area (far left). Not only do they make your space appear larger and lighter, but their reflection also adds an extra dimension of interest.

To create a naturally balanced living environment, it is necessary that the five elements of wood, water, fire, earth, and metal be represented (left). Here, the wooden table, candles, stone holders, and mats, flatware, and water glasses fit the bill perfectly.

In order to negate the harsh rigidity of the modern world, where technological equipment dominates, it is important that you balance hard lines with soft curves to create a more conducive environment in your home (above).

33

A potentially harsh monochrome color theme (below) is softened thanks to a collection of natural objects that have been arranged on the shelf above the fireplace. The vertical arrangement of driftwood balances the horizontal cluster of shells, while the circular pattern on the pillow softens the look even more.

It is perfectly possible to use pattern (right) without making your space look overly busy. Here, the large floor cushions—made from vintage kimonos—provide an ideal complement for the bouffant spray of blossom arranged in an elegant vase.

furniture and decorative accessories in your home, it is possible to improve your relationships, spiritual development, health, and finances.

Although it is extremely fashionable to employ the services of a feng shui expert, it is also possible to correct the flow of energy in your home without the aid of a professional. Not only are there numerous books

An uncluttered bedroom is essential for getting the best out of your downtime (below). Here, the simple furnishings are prevented from appearing bland, thanks to an inspired palette, which contrasts pink, yellow, and gray-blue to create an ultimately restful effect. In addition, the pastel-colored picture makes a powerful statement without appearing too forceful.

decorate your space for health, harmony, and happiness

on the subject, but the basic principles are reasonably straightforward—and will go a long way toward the creation of a spontaneously vital environment. Use the following pointers to balance energy in the home.

• Avoid putting your bed under a window: this will disrupt the energies around you and cause your sleep to become disturbed.
• Arrange sofas and chairs to form a square, as L-shaped layouts are inauspicious.
• Large mirrors are excellent for enhancing energy in a small space. However, do not place a mirror on a wall that reflects the door, as this will dissipate energy.
• Balance straight lines with curves to soften the technological blow of the modern world.
• Place quartz crystals (considered the aspirins of feng shui) on sharp edges, such as the corner of a desk, to dissipate bad chi.
• Open two windows in two different rooms at least twice a week. This way you will enable fresh yang air to sweep away stale yin air.
• While fresh flowers bring yang energy into living spaces, they can also become depressingly yin once they wither. Replace fading flowers with fresh ones as soon as they start to lose their vitality.

The different sizes and shapes of the alcoves carved into the wall (far right) **provide the perfect framework for a collection of exquisite** ceramics. **In addition, their colors create pleasing contrasts of light and shade against the white wall.**

Images of a similar style—be they prints, photographs, or postcards—look great clustered together (above). Make sure that each is simply framed—and remember that arty images do not need to be hanging on a wall to create a striking effect; overlapping postcards, propped up on a windowsill, can be just as arresting. The rough texture of the pebbles provides a calming complement to the clean, smooth finish of the frames, while their organic shapes and varying sizes contrast with the rigid style and identical proportions of the three images.

THE ART OF OBJECT ARRANGEMENT

The creative arrangement of objects is an excellent way of achieving harmonious yin and yang energy in your home. Better still, a small collection of everyday items, such as flowers, fruit, or shells, is preferable to expensive purchased ones because their impact is wrought by their intrinsic beauty, rather than through a contrived and artificial display. Votive candles, shells, and pebbles look their best when clustered together. Choose soft colors and pure shapes that relate well to one another and to the space around them—a jade Buddha next to a white plate, for example. Displaying similar objects in varying degrees of size is also effective—a collection of three baskets in large, medium, and small, for instance; or use this approach for displaying vases, glasses, bowls, and framed prints.

Objects displayed within the natural framework of an alcove or fireplace present another aesthetic choice, while contrasting textures and forms—a rough piece of driftwood with a smooth pebble, or a cashmere throw draped across the back of an upright chair—make for perennially attractive combinations.

Balance is also important, although layout does not have to be regimental. Even numbers create a calming symmetry, while odd numbers add interest. Varying the color and height of objects also works well: juxtapose strong, dark colors with lighter, more translucent ones, or place a couple of tall vases with a few mid-height jars to create an interesting perspective.

When it comes to picture-hanging, a more rigid approach is required. If you have a good-sized wall, hang one large picture in the exact center and leave it at that. Alternatively, a set of prints by the same artist looks great hanging in a group, as long as each is similarly framed. If you choose to hang pictures by different artists, try to keep within the same family of colors, and allow them to breathe by giving each image adequate wall space.

Natural objects, such as shells, pebbles, and seed pods, are preferable to man-made pieces, thanks to their ability to evoke memories of walks along a sandy beach or time spent in a sunlit garden. Contrasting rough textures with smooth ones is a tried-and-tested formula for a pleasing space, and is beautifully illustrated by two shells set together (left)—one showing its shiny interior expanse, the other its grainier exterior. Similarly, the glass jars and lacquered dish (below) soften the coarser surface of the wood-plank table, while the rough pumice stones (below left) contrast with a work surface that has been finished in smooth ceramic tiles.

Autumn leaves laid across a coarsely woven runner (above) make a simple table decoration. The intrinsic beauty of found objects cannot be imitated by artificial means.

A simple rustic-style glass-front cabinet (right) makes an ideal display case for a collection of objects in earthy shades. Pleasing contrasts in height, texture, and shape combine to create an ultimately sophisticated result.

THE THEORY balance and form

A CORNER FOR CONTEMPLATION

In tandem with the ever-increasing pace of the world comes a desire to find fundamental meaning in our lives through the ritual of contemplation. As a result, personal shrines are becoming a popular way for homeowners to find peace and reconnect with their spiritual selves.

The secret of creating a shrine is to find a quiet place where you can meditate for at least fifteen minutes a day. If your home is large enough, set aside one room in which to meditate. If not, furnish a quiet corner with a floor cushion and table on which to display significant objects. These should include representations of the five elements. Ideas include: a feather to symbolize the uplifting effect of air; a filled vase or bowl to symbolize the cleansing properties of water; a candle to symbolize the transforming aspect of fire; sand, salt, or stones to symbolize the grounding qualities of earth; and a coin or silver photo frame to symbolize the neutralizing properties of metal.

shrines need to evolve with your spiritual growth

Your eyes and heart will tell you when you have selected the right balance of objects. Over time, you may find that some of your treasures appear to lose their vitality and need to be replaced. This is because shrines represent your spiritual growth and so must evolve as you do. For example, the treasured collection of shells you picked up on a beach in Bali may become less important if you take another vacation to an equally magical place. Similarly, a token given to you by a loved one will lose its effect if your relationship cools. As a result, it's important to spend time tending your shrine, since this mirrors your attitude toward your spiritual development.

Your area of contemplation (this page) **should contain up to a dozen of your favorite objects, and may include a figurine or image of a deity. The five elements—earth, water, fire, metal, and wood—should also be represented to create a calming balance of yin and yang. It is advisable to include a flower or plant, which will encourage spiritual growth and help you to connect with the natural world.**

Even the most mundane corner of your home (opposite) **can take on a shrinelike quality of calm through the thoughtful selection and placement of ornaments.**

THE DIVINE IS IN THE DETAIL

Thanks to their intrinsic qualities, the most inspiring objects often derive from the world of nature. The bloom of a peach or the beauty of a tightly furled bud are a source of wonder, even though their appearance may be imperfect. In addition, these details are often rich in personal association—a feather found on vacation or a pebble picked up from a windswept beach both have a significance that goes far beyond material value.

The meticulous decor of the tranquil living space is perfect for sharpening our powers of observation, allowing us to perceive the beauty in everyday objects that might be overlooked in a more cluttered environment. For example, a collection of shells simply displayed in a glass dish can evoke the mystical energy of the moon and sea, as does a silvery piece of flotsam that has been weathered by time and tide. Similarly, old wooden furniture that has been polished to a high sheen enables us to appreciate its texture, grain, and flaws, as well as giving us a reassuring sense of stability and comfort through its age-old associations with nobility, wisdom, and strength. By the same token, hand-thrown ceramics, carvings hewn from grainy wood, and lovingly embroidered rugs all have a similar intuitive appeal. Because we know they have been created with care and attention, we appreciate the unique irregularities that give each piece its own identity.

It is not necessary to create an elaborate display in order to reap the beneficial effects of flowers—a single stem placed in a drinking glass (far left) will enhance your living space just as effectively.

A pared-down decor allows us to appreciate the beauty of a few treasured objects (left). Here, the polished sheen of an antique chest highlights the grain of the wood, while the impact of the decorative egg-shaped ornament is enhanced by the elegantly spare lines of the modern lamp beside it.

An almost perfectly symmetrical display (below) of two framed photographs and a pair of oak plinths is cleverly completed by the contrasting shapes of the two substantial beeswax candles.

Flowers are a beautiful and inspiring way to introduce natural details into the home. Not only are they exquisite to look at, but they also encourage spiritual awakening and generate energy. The most effective include chrysanthemum to help concentrate the mind; lotus to open channels of spiritual consciousness; iris to promote spiritual integration; rose for love; black-eyed Susan to awaken spiritual consciousness; angels' trumpets to promote spiritual initiation; and angelica for guidance from divine realms.

appreciate the beauty in natural details and found objects

Polished stones or gemstones have been used on altars for thousands of years in the belief that each releases a unique energy. Stones that exude particular spiritual powers include emeralds for healing; lapis lazuli for intuition; bloodstone for strength; quartz crystals for attunement; and rubies for strength, health, and spiritual passion.

ETERNAL FLAMES

For thousands of years, candles were an essential part of everyday life—illuminating dark nights and representing faith and hope in religious rituals across the world. Today, candlelight is an important feature in the home, representing the divine spark within each of us and helping to ignite our imaginations through the magical evocation of shadows.

There are numerous types of candles available on the market. Good options for use in meditation or the creation of a tranquil and calming atmosphere include colored flowers that float in water, sculptural blocks with four or five wicks apiece, and elegant beeswax tapers, which promote a churchlike feel when pushed

Contrast the waxy texture of candles with rough stone holders and glassy pebbles, and opt for scented varieties as the use of fragrance enhances peaceful feelings. Aromatherapy also comes in the form of incense sticks, which are currently back in fashion, and offer a simple way to imbue your living space with spiritual feelings as well as adding a hint of exotica.

into a bowl of sand. Similarly, small votive candles in colored glass containers give an incandescent glow, while a cluster of votives creates a galaxy of seemingly divine illuminations.

DIVINE FRAGRANCE

Known to boost our sense of wellbeing, the use of fragrance can help us to turn our homes into havens of sensory perception, creating an uplifting environment when we need to be stimulated, and a calming one when relaxation is called for. Better still, the choice of olfactory products on offer is guaranteed to lift the

spirits, providing sweet-smelling aromas in the form of vaporizers, candles, potpourri, herb-filled pillows, joss sticks, and incense cones.

Scented candles are the most popular way to fragrance your space; you can even opt for the feng shui variety, which offer the essences of fire, water, metal, earth, and air in elegant wax columns. Aromatherapy candles scented with jasmine, orange blossom, frangipani, honeysuckle, and lily of the valley are also effective mood-enhancers, while spicy-smelling candles imbue the atmosphere with the exotic scents of amber, musk, and cinnamon.

Floating candles shaped like flower heads and combined with petals and blooms are an attractive and effective way to introduce the Zen elements of water and fire into your home (left and below). Reminiscent of age-old meditative practices in the Far East, candlelight helps to promote feelings of spiritual attunement.

Sleekly packaged beeswax candles (left) will burn to fill the room with a subtle but distinctive aroma.

An arrangement of inexpensive votive candles neatly set inside a selection of colorful Moroccan tea glasses (right) will give your living space an incandescent glow, helping to ignite the imagination and generate spiritual energy.

As the fashion for candlelight continues to gather pace, so too does the choice of wax illuminations on offer. Whether you choose to light your home with elegant beeswax tapers or sculptural blocks with five or six wicks apiece (below), candlelight helps infuse the atmosphere with calming or uplifting aromas as well as creating evocative shadows.

use aromas to encourage feelings of optimism and goodwill

Essential oils are another favorable way to scent your home, thanks to their efficacy at clearing unwanted vibrations. Most potent when they come into contact with heat, vaporizers such as oil burners, electric diffusers, or ceramic rings—that fit around lightbulbs—emit the fragrance of essential oils gently and consistently. To create an ultimately soulful ambience, try sandalwood for spiritual attunement, frankincense for spiritual clarity, and cedar wood for clearing spiritual energies. To soothe the senses, choose geranium, neroli, rose, jasmine, ylang ylang, lavender, or camomile.

For thousands of years, humans have burned herbs, scented wood resins, and other aromatic substances in order to connect with the spirit world through the meditative practice of watching smoke spiral heavenward. Popular in the hippy-trippy 1960s and 1970s, the fashion for insence sticks is back in vogue, thanks to a renewed desire for spiritual attunement. These days, however, burning incense is an altogether more sophisticated affair: sleek lacquered boxes replace the plastic packets of yesteryear, while scents such as lemongrass and ginger replace the staple aromas of the past—jasmine and patchouli.

Space, light, and natural
materials have been used
to full effect (left) in order to
create the ultimate in spiritual
chic. The power of contrast is
also exploited, with the smooth
concrete of the curvilinear
passage juxtaposed against
a wall of untreated wood and
the rigid lines of the windows.

A variety of natural materials
has been used to create a
restful corner (right), that is
both comfortable and aesthetic.

natural connection

The interaction of organic textures and colors in the home
creates an environment that is as spontaneous as it is serene.

*as does the interactions of natural environmental processes that support and
are supported by each other to create the necessary functional systems
in the home.*

Furnishing your home with natural elements is a Zen tradition that is successfully
applied in any home seeking to provide sanctuary from the outside world. Materials
such as wood, stone, linen, and hemp allow us to energize our spaces through the
fecundity of the earth and to revel in their rich textures and colors. According to the
dictates of Zen living, natural materials stimulate the senses in a way that synthetic
ones cannot. Compare, for example, the merits of a cold linoleum floor with a warm
wooden style, and the more attractive option is easy to spot. Similarly, a smooth
glass door handle is much more tactile than a tacky plastic one.

By the same token, these criteria for spiritual living are also in tune with the
current fashion for eco-chic—a furnishing style that is environmentally friendly and
concentrates on the use of organic materials to create a truly soulful space. Homes

*also natural materials expose us to things we are built to handle, have more
to give that is positive on many more levels than does synthetic?*

49

Texture and pattern are needed in the peaceful home to prevent the space from appearing spartan or bland. An occasional splash of red, combined with fabric furnishings upholstered in bold checks, gives the simple log cabin (opposite) an immediate injection of energy, while the smooth lines of the sofa (right) contrast with the textured flooring and a patterned throw to give a calming sense of balance. Similarly, the reflective sheen of the polished terracotta tiles (below) provides a cool complement to the warmer appearance of the natural-fiber matting with jute edging.

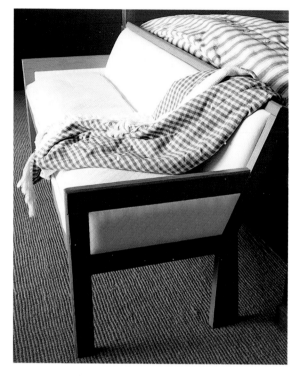

that are lacking in natural elements will cause their owners to become spiritually deprived—increasing their sense of isolation from the great outdoors.

As far as furniture design is concerned, organic curves are preferable to straight ones, simply because they help us to escape from the rigidity of modern technology where hard lines and sharp corners predominate. That said, if you do choose to take a hard line with your furniture, it is possible to temper

in a pared-down space, contrast of texture is vital for preventing your home from becoming bland

Nature itself is an interacting collection of multi layered patterns and dynamics.

the look of straight-up-and-down sofas, chairs, and footstools through the use of fabrics. Sumptuous upholstery, squashy pillows and casually draped throws—preferably with fringe around the edges—will all reduce the hard appearance of strictly linear furniture. Similarly, the introduction of pattern will also help to divert attention away from sharp edges; choose bold checks, faded florals, or sassy stripes for a look that is spontaneous and informal. The canny use of color is another effective deflector: natural shades such as mulberry, tan, and terracotta create the illusion of a calming and coherent whole, while more vibrant colors such as red, purple, turquoise, pink, and yellow create arresting focal points.

THE THEORY natural connection

Far from appearing cold and unyielding, the dark flagstones on the floor (this page) have been softened thanks to the bold expanse of orange paint on the wall. A slighter brighter variation of traditional terracotta, this color also helps lift the pedestrian design of the wooden table and draws attention to the plant pots on the windowsill.

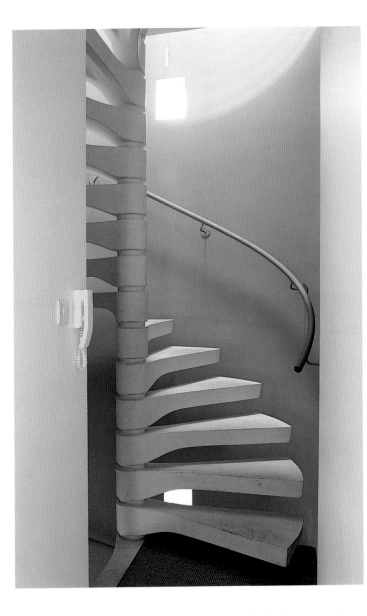

COLOR YOURSELF CALM

The colors of nature are a prime inspiration in the spiritual home. In order to create a spontaneously calming ambience, combine base shades with earth ones before seasoning with a splash of sea-blue or a flick of forest green.

Base colors include subtle shades of white veering towards cream, beige, straw, ocher, and sand; these can be combined with soft pastels such as pale blues or washes of green for an ultimately soothing effect. Where contrast is required, earth colors, drawn from rocks and soils, are applied. These shades are muted and subtle, varying from the cool whites, grays, and pinks of marble, slate, and granite, through the yellow tones of desert sands to the warmer rusts and deep reds of monumental rocks.

SPIRITUAL SHADES

Brown Brown creates feelings of solidity and protection through its association with the colour of earth – pigments such as "sienna," "umber," and "ochre" are literally made from earth. Use it in a newly decorated room to create a warm, lived-in feel. Brown should be used sparingly, however; too much can cause feelings of depression.

Beige and oatmeal These neutral colors sit well with organic materials such as wood, cane, wicker, and stone. Effective stress-busters, beige

In order to create a sense of coherence, it is important to make sure transitional spaces such as passages, landings, and stairs continue the serene theme. The mystical shade of the blue paint on the stairwell (above) is an excellent example and illustrates how a simple

wash of color can promote spiritual feelings of lightness and transcendence.

The muted hues of glazed bottles (right) summon up soft shades of nature, evoking images of green meadows, calm seas, and heather-filled moors.

Instead of man-made materials, choose natural ones, such as a feather fan (left), in order to give your home a sense of genuine soul.

A cool green hall (below) is perfect for creating a smooth link between the upstairs living area and the downstairs one. Known for its perfect balance of yin and yang, green is the ideal color for transitional areas within the home.

The warm earthy palette in a light-filled bedroom (opposite) creates a naturally restful mood as well as helping to make it appear more spacious. In addition, a neutral color scheme provides the perfect backdrop for the natural wood furnishings and Native American artwork.

choose a palette of natural, earthy tones, injecting accents of soft blues, greens, or reds into a neutral backdrop

and oatmeal are both easy to live with. In addition, these pale neutrals reflect light, making your space feel bigger and brighter.

Terracotta This rich earth color is warm and intense, and has served as a staple furnishing shade for hundreds of years. As a result, terracotta has a timeless feel and creates a feeling of primitive vibrancy without being overbearing.

Blue Arguably the most spiritual color of the spectrum, blue triggers the release of eleven tranquillizing hormones in the body. It is also linked to the spirituality of the moon, together with white, silver, and indigo.

Green Green symbolizes regeneration and spiritual growth. Not only is it restful on the eyes, it also contains equal proportions of yin and yang, helping to balance energy and promote harmony.

Violet Violet calms the spirit at its deepest level. It also helps soothe the body and mind, and is often used in meditation rooms.

Yellow Yellow buoys the spirit and engenders feelings of optimism. It is also one of the most effective ways to brighten a room that is deprived of natural light.

The cohesive and pristine appearance of pale wooden floorboards, wooden window frames, and a long plank table (opposite) is saved from blandness, thanks to the reflective sheen of the polished floor and the uneven edge of the table.

Offering the perfect corner for contemplation, the ultimate organic seat (above) has been carved from an age-old tree trunk and fits into its curvy setting with reassuring solidity.

Knotted and whorled with age, the planks that make up the log cabin (left) offer enough interest and variation to sustain wall-to-ceiling coverage.

TREE OF LIFE

Throughout history, trees have been viewed as the axis through which divine energy flows from the supernatural world to the natural one. As a result, it's hardly surprising that wood is a key element in a spiritual space, helping to promote feelings of stability and comfort through its age-old associations with nobility and strength. When wood is young and green, it exudes energy and growth. As it gets older and more seasoned, it becomes imbued with wisdom and spirituality, lending credence to the ancient belief that each tree has its own soul. Better still, there are numerous varieties of wood on the market, each offering its own brand of color, scent, texture, and grain. Different woods summon different atmospheres. For example, if you want to create a calming feel, opt for pale light-reflecting lumber such as bleached driftwood or golden pine. A homey ambience is best achieved with richly colored woods that add warmth and security; while dark woods such as time-worn oak or gleaming ebony promote safe feelings of intimacy and seclusion.

The walnut-faced bentwood arms that wrap the classic butterfly-shaped chair (above) in a graceful embrace also provide a smooth contrast to the darker, more deeply engrained seat and back, and prevent the design from appearing too spindly.

Offering a funky alternative to conventional flagstones, pebbles embedded in a concrete bathroom floor (below) conjure up breezy beach walks. Conversely, the bamboo panel evokes an Eastern feel—the unusual combination puts a fresh spin on bringing the outside indoors.

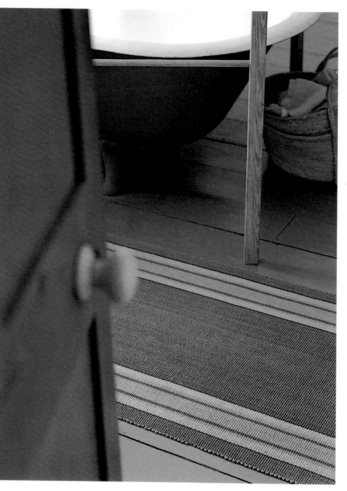

A blue-and-cream-striped flatweave cotton runner (left) gives the gray floorboards of a peacefully spartan bathroom a new lease on life.

Wooden boards present an endlessly streamlined flooring option and provide the perfect base for contrasting different textures such as this abaca rug (below) overlaid with woven wool that has been felted and shrunk.

A white concrete floor with a single-stripe detail of cobblestones provides the ideal base for a minimalist bedroom with an exotic feel (opposite).

GETTING GROUNDED

Thanks to their calming linearity, wooden boards are a great way to spiritualize your space. Better still, they can be employed in a variety of ways to create different looks within the home. Use them on your floors, walls, and ceilings to create the intimacy of a cozy log cabin, or whitewash dark boards to open out small interiors and create a feeling of lightness and expansion. The continuous appearance of stripped boards also works brilliantly with wooden furniture carved from a different grain or hue, providing a textural contrast that is spontaneous and natural.

If wooden boards are not a possibility for flooring, try laying compressed bamboo instead. Not only is this wood strong and durable, but it is also water-resistant and aesthetically pleasing. Alternative "green" flooring includes cork, which is also waterproof as well as being inexpensive and naturally sustainable, and wool felt, which is hardwearing and offers excellent sound insulation.

stone is imbued with feelings of strength, solidity, and stability

Mixing and matching different types of stone is a great way to showcase the variations available. The combination of hard slate with soft sandstone (opposite), together with a couple of sea-molded rocks, creates a soothing symphony of color, shape, and texture.

If you can afford stone flagging (left), choose the largest pavers you can find, in order to create a feeling of smooth serenity.

The vogue for natural materials has prompted a revival in one of the oldest forms of flooring known to man—rush matting. Also available in jute, sisal, coir, and seagrass, these fibrous coverings work well, thanks to their organic texture, earthy colors, and adherence to the Zen dictate of combining form with function.

ROCK OF AGES

Given its seeming immutability, it's not surprising that stone is linked to the building of sacred structures such as temples, cathedrals, and shrines. By the same token, its qualities of permanence and tradition make stone a quintessential feature in contemporary interiors.

The popular image of stone—cool, pale, and smooth—is belied by its wonderful variety of colors, textures, and patterns. Capable of appearing fresh and inviting or warm and earthy, stone helps to "ground" your home in a number of ways, depending on the state of your finances. For example, the spiritual homeowner with a healthy bank balance should consider laying flagstone paving in his or her hall, living area, or bathroom, while less expensive options include installing marble counters in the kitchen or a limestone sink or terrazzo tiles in the bathroom. Even a terracotta urn or a vase filled with pebbles will help to imbue your space with the mysticism of age-old rock.

Complete with a wonderfully fine linear grain, the silky-smooth organic curves of a sinuous chaise longue in teak wood (this page) are further emphasized by its more solid branchlike supports.

Contrasting a variety of natural textures is a simple way to create a haven of sensory pleasure with seemingly little effort. A shorn sheepskin floor rug complements the unfinished edges of the roughly hewn wood lounger (below).

The distressed appearance of an old painted wooden table, combined with fibrous placemats and the gently curving edges of a smooth stone bowl (right), creates a soft and calming display—perfect for relaxed dining.

NATURAL FABRICS TO SOOTHE THE SENSES

Resilient and attractive, the texture and drape of natural fabrics is almost impossible to imitate by artificial means. Linen, cotton, and wool can be woven or knitted into many different looks—from rough and rugged to gossamer-fine and floaty. This versatility brings the textiles of our homes into harmony with nature, helping to suggest warmth in winter and coolness in summer.

In addition, most natural fabrics are able to withstand years of use, often becoming more attractive with age. Old linen sheets that have softened over time feel much nicer than starchy new ones, while the soft patina of a faded silk quilt invokes the atmosphere of a bygone era. Integrity and quality are key when it comes to choosing fabrics for the home: opt for the softest cashmere, the finest cotton, and the supplest suede to please the senses.

Pillows in different colors, patterns, and textures (far left) are an effective way to jazz up and bring comfort to a pared-down space. Here, the heathery hues of the woven wool and herringbone tweed introduce a rustic look. In contrast, the gossamer softness of the mohair throw (left) adds an instantly luxurious element to spartan interiors.

Juxtaposing similar textures can be equally effective. On a natural-fiber flooring, similarly upholstered stool seats (below) compound the organic look.

TOUCHY-FEELY TEXTURE AND CONTRAST

One of the best ways to achieve contrast is by following the law of opposites—an effective method that works especially well if the rooms in your home revolve around a single color.

Hard and soft

Polished pebbles in a sisal container

A wrought-iron daybed with a fleece-covered mattress

A glass container planted with a feathery fern

Rough and smooth

Coir matting with suede floor cushions

An untreated wooden shelf supporting a row of glass jars

A wicker laundry basket in a marble bathroom

Warm and cool

Leather upholstery on a metal chair

A sheepskin rug on a stone floor

A bright print in a stainless-steel frame

With its complementary mix of horizontal and vertical lines, the decor of the room (this page) achieves a pleasingly balanced whole without appearing contrived. The streamlined appearance of the wooden flooring is echoed in the horizontal lines of the chair's leather upholstery, while various shallow bowls decorate the top shelves of the alcove. This is balanced by a collection of tall vases on the shelves below, and a chunky tribal necklace that has been draped over the top of the door.

Straight and curved

A streamlined hall with a spiral staircase

A rectangular vase filled with twisted willow twigs

A square table with a round lamp

Luxurious and rigorous

A raw-silk cushion on a stone seat

A sinuous vase on a concrete plinth

A mohair throw on a straight-backed sofa

Patterned and plain

Pique towels in a glass shower cubicle

Exposed brick walls with lacquered shelves

A bouclé sofa with nubuck cushions

LIFE-AFFIRMING FLOWERS

In the future, trend predictors believe that urban dwellers with no access to a garden will devote a room to live greenery in a bid to reconnect with nature. Whether the idea of a "green room" actually catches on is irrelevant in the spiritual home—the inclusion of plants and flowers is a fundamental feature that cannot be overlooked. One of the reasons for this is the Zen belief that plants introduce the element of wood, which signifies growth and development, and helps to promote spiritual wellbeing.

watching a bud reveal a flower or a new leaf
unfurl keeps us in touch with the cycle of nature

Flowers are also the most beautiful and subtle way to scent the home. Fill your space with sweet-smelling roses, narcissi, freesias, and hyacinths, or plant fragrant shrubs, such as jasmine or honeysuckle, close to your window so the scent washes through. Herbs are also wonderfully aromatic: bergamot, lavender, mint, rosemary, sage, and thyme give off the nicest smells and can be grown in windowboxes or indoor pots.

The medicinal properties of plants are well documented: use the herbs in your garden to make your own simple tonics, such as herbal teas, for example. Leafy plants also benefit your environment by purifying the air—drawing in carbon dioxide and replenishing it with oxygen, as well as releasing moisture to prevent your space becoming too dry. In addition, it has been proven that certain house plants can filter the environmental toxins produced by computers and printers, as well as those pollutants caused by cigarette smoke and chemical cleaners. The best purifying plants to include in your space are gerberas, moth orchids, tulips, cyclamens, chrysanthemums, peace lilies, areca palms, spider plants, bamboo palms, and rubber plants.

Whether you're a rose fanatic, a herb grower, or an ardent horticulturalist, flowers and greenery are vital in the peaceful home, fulfilling a number of criteria to help enhance the feel-good factor of your living environment. Not only are flowers beautiful to look at, but their scent is the subtlest way to fragrance the air. The presence of living greenery also promotes energy and optimism, while leafy plants are one of the most effective ways to purify the atmosphere, drawing in carbon dioxide and replacing it with oxygen.

"Beauty springs from thought and sensibility, rather than from material wealth."

Claudio Silverstrin (1954–)

PART TWO

the space

The unique layout of the living space (right) combines weathered wood with faded bricks and earthy tones to create a homey feel, despite the proportions of the room. In addition, the generous array of cushions transforms the cool slate steps into an area for total relaxation, while the low-level coffee table adds a laidback lounge feel.

living

It is important to create a living space that is conducive to good relations: calm and uncluttered on one hand, comfortable and inviting on the other.

This is the main room of the home, and for this reason your living area is likely to be a hub of social activity—a place where family and friends gather together to exchange news, gossip, and ideas. The alternative facet of your living space is its function as a "quiet room." This is, after all, the home's premier chill-out zone— a place where you can listen to music, talk on the phone, watch films, or simply cogitate on your life.

The primary function of the decor you choose for your living space, like other rooms in the home, is to convey a sense of serenity. The best way to achieve it is to surround yourself with colors and textures that please and calm you. In addition, choose shapes that are easy to live with and try to maintain a harmonious balance between form and function, because this room—by its very nature—is likely to be busier than others in the home.

KICK BACK AND RELAX

In order to maximize the spiritual potential of the living room, aim to create an airy ambience in which to kick back and relax. One of the best ways to promote a spacious look is through the use of natural flooring. Whether you choose coir matting

The exotica of heavy Eastern furnishings sit calmly and comfortably alongside traditional Western ones, thanks to the symmetrical and formal arrangement of this room. The red-and-cream color scheme, which is repeated throughout the space, compounds the sense of order, while the differing sizes of the pots on the cabinets (below) play a quirky trick on our sense of perspective.

or flagstones, an organic base will go a long way toward making your home appear more grounded. As far as the spiritual space is concerned, wood planks are ideal, providing a linear look that is both calming and cohesive. If you're not lucky enough to have floorboards in your home, consider investing in reclaimed planks or in the less expensive option of laminate woodstrip, because a base of wood beneath your feet is one of the most effective ways to create a spiritual feel.

Although wooden flooring can feel like a ubiquitous feature in modern interiors, the variety of choice—in terms of color, texture, grain, and finish—means that wood is easily adapted to create a number of different looks. For example, stripped and polished boards give a rustic ambience; whitewashed boards produce an airy romantic feel; dark-stained boards make your space seem safe and intimate; while polished parquet or beech-strip flooring is clean and contemporary.

a big couch is a key feature of the living space, especially if your home's style is pared down with minimal fabric furnishings

Although the peaceful space errs toward minimalism, it is a far cry from the spartan principles of Zen living. Instead, fabrics are sybaritic in the extreme (this page), and cozy cashmere throws combine with natural materials for textural contrast.

Maximize the peaceful potential of your living space by using colors and textures that mesh harmoniously together (opposite). A neutral palette in warm shades; fabrics that strike an easy balance between form and function; and ornaments to provide soothingly aesthetic focal points will all create an ultimately conducive ambience for relaxation.

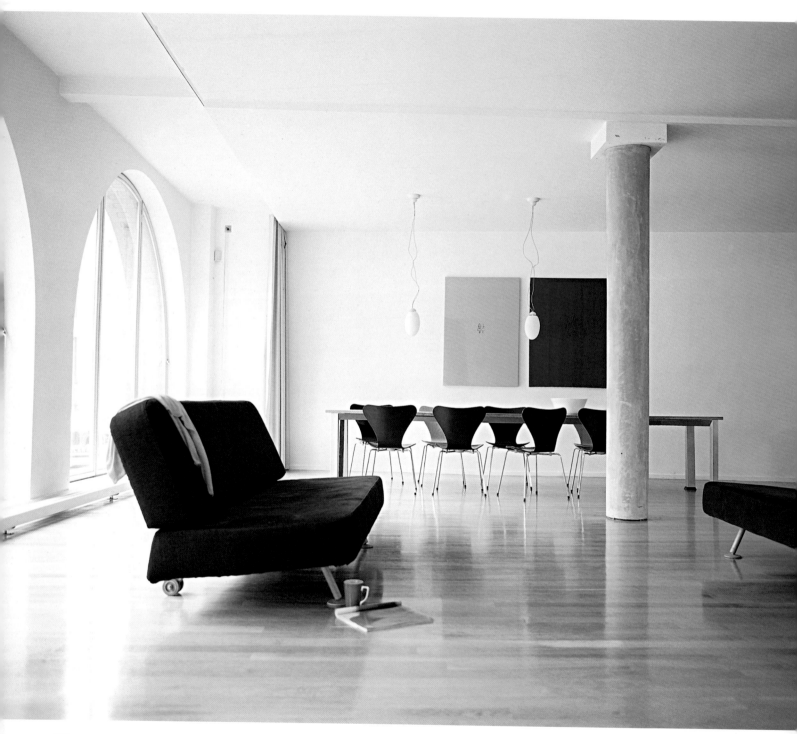

LAYOUTS FOR CLEAN LIVING

It is likely that there will be more furniture in your living space than elsewhere in the home, so it is important to consider the relationship between the individual pieces carefully. The proportions of the room, of course, will need to be taken into account—a vast loft apartment, for example, can accommodate several large pieces of furniture without the overall effect appearing too cluttered. However, a harmony of shape, color, and texture must also be established. This is achieved simply, by balancing hard lines with soft curves, pale shades with brighter ones, and smooth surfaces with rough finishes. In this way, you will create an aesthetic balance of yin and yang which, in turn, allows a free flow of cosmic energy throughout your space.

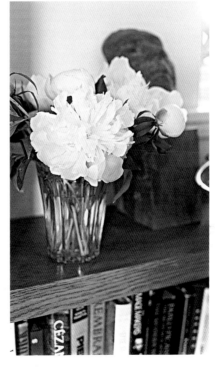

Despite their scale, the streamlined style of the sofas and chairs in the loft apartment (opposite) creates a feeling of lightness and space, and this is compounded by the navy-and-white color scheme.

A favorite comfy armchair upholstered in a luxurious fabric, such as raspberry-colored velvet (far left), will maximize the comfort-zone effect. Add a glass of soft blooms (left) to complete your sensory enjoyment.

Despite being complementary colors, red and green used together as the dominant colors in a room could jar the senses. However, soft pink against a jade-green couch (above) makes a restful and welcoming combination.

warm honey colors usher in feelings of comfort and hospitality

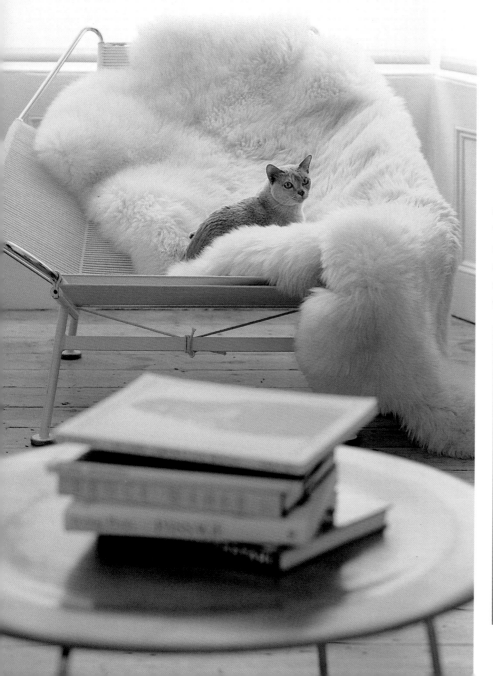

KEEP COLORS NEUTRAL

The key to creating a spiritual color scheme is to find a color or group of colors with which you feel at peace, and then to work with them as a base. Any pale shade—as long as it is clear and tonal—will provide a soothing backdrop, although for the living area, neutrals are often the first choice.

As long as your chairs and tables are of a similar hue, it is possible to mix and match furnishing styles, combining contemporary designs with outmoded ones while still retaining a cohesive feel. In addition, a neutral palette allows for the addition of almost any other color, and contrasts particularly well with white, cream, violet, and every shade of blue—from indigo to turquoise and aquamarine to duck's egg.

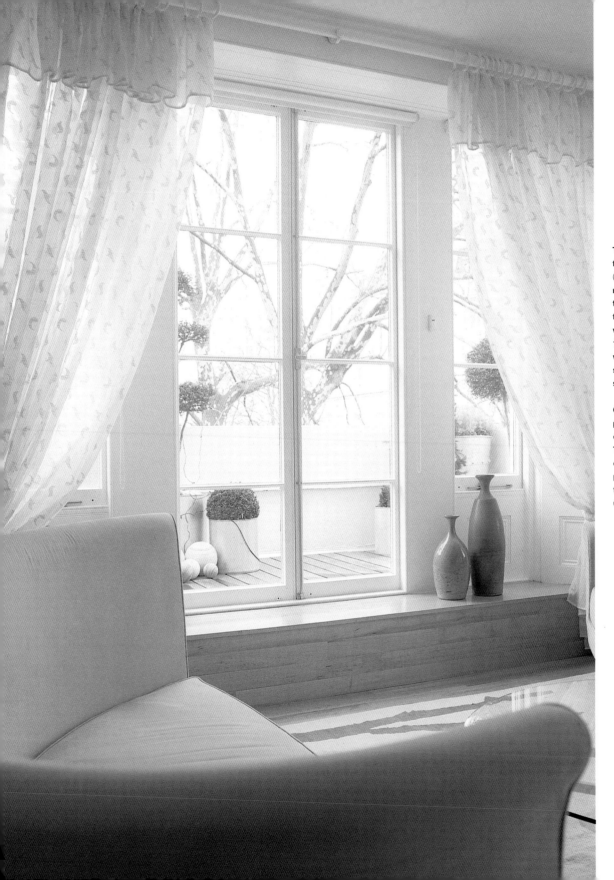

The warm whites and honey tones of the living space (opposite) allow for an eclectic mix of designs that combine to make a peaceful whole. The traditional shutters contrast with the 1960s bubble TV and 1950s steel-and-rope chair, while the spartan layout is softened by the addition of a sumptuous sheepskin throw.

Opting for a basically neutral palette allows for the addition of almost any other color. The lemon yellow of the gently curved sofa (this page) is a perfect example, compounding the sunny feel of a bright and uplifting living space.

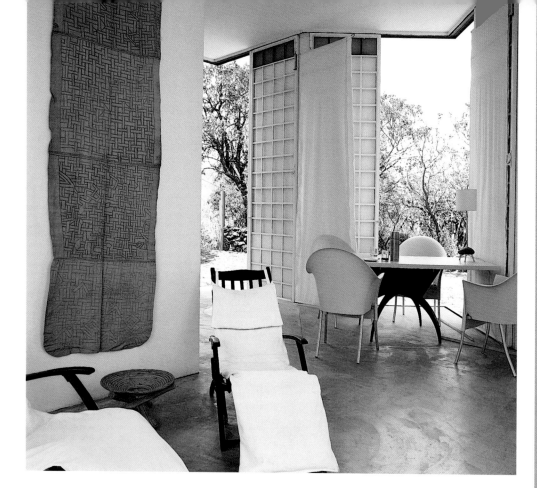

SOFTLY, SOFTLY FURNISHINGS

Your living-room sofa will be one of the most used pieces of furniture in your home. So, because you will be spending so much time lounging around on it, finding the right one requires thorough and persistent research. Once you find a style you like, remember to sit on it for at least five minutes in order to test its quality. If you can feel the springs or the frame poking through, eliminate it immediately and move on to a different make. It is also important that you check potential seating for adequate spinal support—a squishy sofa may feel great for sinking into when you kick off your shoes after a hard day, but a style that is too soft is likely to cause postural problems in the long term.

The presence of comfortable sofas and chairs in your living space also provides the ideal opportunity to create a restrained feeling of decadence through the addition of luxurious details. For example, upholster your sofa in plush velvet to promote a laidback lounger's feel, or scatter a daybed with pillows covered in super-soft cashmere

Whether you're looking for a huge squashy sofa, a sumptuously spacious armchair, or an elegant lounger (above), finding the perfect seating for your living space demands time and effort to find a style that looks good, but compromises nothing in comfort.

A simply elegant sofa plus a collection of generous-sized rattan chairs mean the occupants of this pristine living space (right) can lounge or entertain in comfort.

Although the styles of the chair and sofa are different (far left), the patterned upholstery in varying green checks creates a calming link.

You don't have to stick to a pale palette to create a peaceful look. Strong colors that have faded with time are just as effective (below), and mean a mix of patterns can coexist without appearing overdone.

opting for an uncontrived palette allows for the display of different furnishing styles and for the introduction of pattern

for irresistible comfort. Fabric furnishings also provide an ideal opportunity to inject a jolt of pattern and color into your design scheme. Upholstery in cheerful checks is particularly effective, providing warmth and vibrancy within the calming confines of a regimented pattern. By sticking to one range of colors or type of pattern, textiles can also be used to unify different styles of seating within the living area and to counter the potentially cluttered effect of grouping furniture together.

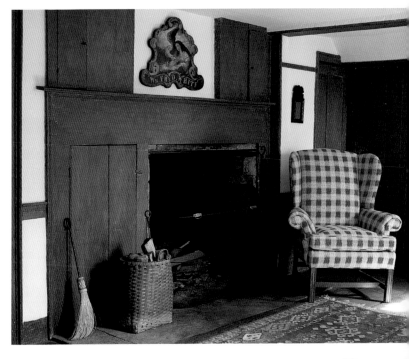

The gently curving back of the wicker sofa (opposite) is complemented by the rigid lines of the chunky paneling, while the regimented arrangement is softened by the distressed surfaces of the faded blue armoire and the sea-green coffee table. Adding a simple bunch of lavender or lilac (above right) from the garden will provide a soothing focal point, as well as filling the room with wonderful aromas.

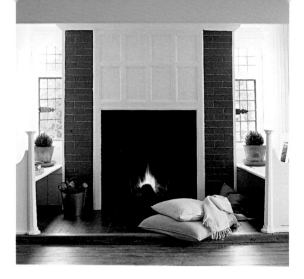

An essentially cool space, with white paneling and bare brickwork, the living area (left) is brought to life by the flickering flames of the fire, which soften the decor and infuse it with an inviting glow.

Continuing the fiery theme, the slate shelf (opposite) is dotted with a a collection of candles in varying shapes and sizes. Not only does this enhance the monochrome design, but it also adds a number of alternative focal points.

the presence of merry, darting flames will imbue your minimalist space with warmth, light, and energy

LIVING LIGHT OF THE HEARTH

A fire flickering in the hearth is one of the most effective ways to enhance the atmosphere of your home—as well as providing warmth and offering a soothing and meditative focal point. A log fire is also fabulously aromatic. Not only is the distinctive smell of burning wood calming and therapeutic, but its natural fragrance can be enhanced in a number of ways. For example, add a handful of pine cones or a bunch of dried herbs for a refreshing top-note, or rub woody essential oils into your logs before burning them, in order to fragrance your space with the scent of cedar wood, cypress, sandalwood, or rosewood.

If your living room does not have a working fireplace, or you live in a city where log fires are prohibited, you might want to consider the installation of a gas version. These fires may not give out much heat, but their lifelike appearance is extremely effective.

Even when your fireplace is not in use—during the summer, for instance—it can still be employed to create a focal point within the room. Simply replace the presence of flickering flames with a still-life display of natural objects: vases of flowers, chunky candles, or a collection of wicker baskets all look great when framed within the parameters of the fireplace, and add an earthy organic feel that compounds the elemental look.

Logs stored haphazardly beside the fireplace (below) add a relaxed rustic feel, in contrast to the grandeur of the antique mirror and delicate stencil work. Bunches of lavender and rosemary are on hand to be thrown into the flames for instant aromatherapy.

Simple wooden knobs combine with rough paintwork (right) for understated interest.

Chunky pottery, scrubbed wood, freestanding furniture, and wicker baskets filled with fruit create a tranquil feel in a rustic-style kitchen (opposite). Compound the look with terracotta paint and pickled floorboards, and use wooden plate racks for dishes to instill a calming sense of order.

eating

Dining simply in the company of family and friends is one of the fastest routes to relaxation, helping to combat stress and raise the spirits.

The impact of food on our spiritual health is manifest in a number of different ways. A nutritious diet enables us to function at optimum efficiency, while the process of converting raw ingredients into tasty aromatic dishes feeds our creative impulses.

There are no hard-and-fast rules regarding the design of the peaceful eating space. That said, the current fashion for a combined cooking and eating area works particularly well in the soul home simply because it provides a feast for the senses: delicious aromas and visual delights whet the appetite, while an open-plan layout provides an homogenized feel, that helps mind, body and soul to stay connected.

As long as your cooking and eating space remains warm and clutter-free, it is possible to create a feeling of wellbeing through the creation of two very different styles. If you're the efficient type, the clean-cut minimalist look is best; if you're earthier and more relaxed, the modern rustic look is likely to be more appropriate.

RUSTIC STYLE

The rustic eating space ushers in feelings of warmth and welcome, and home-cooked meals. Freestanding pieces of furniture are favored over made-to-measure built-in units, while pickled floorboards and terracotta tiles replace cool, hard surfaces such as marble and steel.

That said, the modern rustic look is also pared down, relying on a few thoughtfully chosen pieces to evoke a spontaneous shabby-chic look. A warm-toned wooden table provides a reassuring focal point in the earthy kitchen, while a range, a deep ceramic sink, and a Victorian pine hutch decorated with plates promote a time-honored feel. The idea is to celebrate the intrinsic beauty of antiquated furnishings in order to imbue your cooking and eating area with an authentic and intuitive feel.

Although the peaceful kitchen is pared down, it also allows for features such as open shelving (far left), where the restful shapes of gleaming stainless-steel canisters and pure white bowls enhance, rather than detract from, the overall effect of calm and efficiency.

The super-sleek eating space of the converted loft (center) is softened by a calming palette of soft blues and dove gray. In addition, the pale wooden floor and elegant Eames chairs balance out the harsh concrete ceiling, creating a cohesive look that is efficient without being cold.

Opting for a mixed palette of bright colors need not create a jarring effect. Instead, the structured linearity of the built-in cabinets (left) complements the bold blocks of yellow, pink, and green.

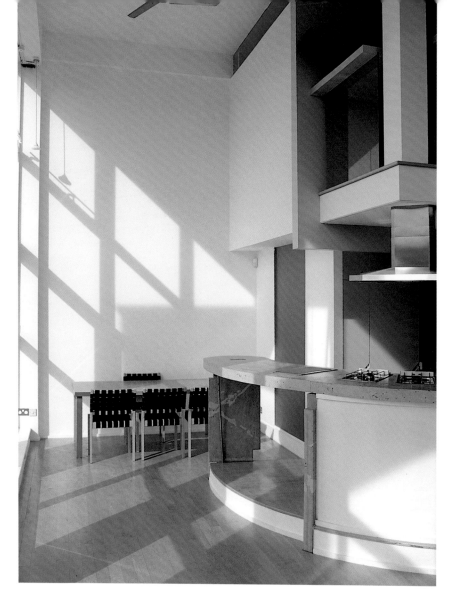

In tune with the relaxed style of the rustic cooking and eating space, color choices are wonderfully wide-ranging. For example, earthy shades of terracotta, sand, buff, beige, and biscuit will help to compound the organic look, while sky blues and forest greens are fresh and upbeat. It is also possible to introduce pattern without impinging on the scrubbed wholesome feel. Contrast duck's egg blue walls with a flower-print tablecloth, for example, or surround an old pine table with simple wood chairs upholstered in bright and cheerful gingham.

WARM AND INTIMATE DETAILS

The rustic cooking/eating space also benefits from a smattering of wholesome accessories. To complete the natural country look, include the following: fresh linen dishtowels; wildflowers displayed in a simple clear-glass vase; woven baskets for storing potatoes and apples; old-fashioned storage jars, battered tin tea caddies, French enamel bread and flour bins; chunky peasant pottery; the occasional sprigged print; and old-fashioned creamware.

ZEN STYLE

If the minimalist look is more your style, then your cooking and eating space should adhere to the Zen aesthetic of combining form with function in order to create an effective culinary environment. As a result, hi-tech elements combine with natural ones to produce a spiritually soothing interior where drawers roll smoothly on their runners, the lights can be dimmed at a touch, and the knives are always sharp.

It goes without saying that the Zen cooking and eating area is perfectly pared down. In direct contrast to the rustic look, sleek units and acres of clean shiny surfaces create a streamlined effect, while all the unattractive but necessary white goods (the washing machine, refrigerator, and dishwasher) are artfully

A great example of Zen style, the cooking and eating area (above) **combines industrial elements with natural ones to create a balanced whole. In addition, the floor-to-ceiling windows mean the space is washed with lots of natural light, while the curve of the counter softens the minimalist look and prevents the space from appearing too spartan.**

Simple glass storage jars (opposite, left) **filled with basic items such as teabags and dried goods add a workaday feel to the streamlined aesthetic of minimalist eating areas.**

Combine plain dishes in soft hues (opposite, right) **with a pair of wooden chopsticks and a linen tablecloth for a naturally aesthetic look.**

Whether you choose ceramics in nature-inspired shades or opt for simple styles lacking in adornment (above), chunky handmade pottery works brilliantly in the rustic- and Zen-style eating space, compounding the no-frills look in a single definitive move.

Contemporary lines and organic elements sit comfortably together within a neutral color scheme (opposite, right). For example, the vertical panels of the wooden units are echoed in the modern artwork on the walls, while the soft circles of the earthenware are picked up by the graphic pattern woven into the rug.

The slightly worn appearance of the metal canisters (right) adds a time-honored feel to a rustic-style kitchen.

disguised behind a facade of calming panels. Surface treatments combine harder finishes of steel, chrome, marble and granite with softer wood tones in warm pale hues, such as beech, maple and cherry wood.

By the same token, colors in the Zen cooking–eating space are also chosen for their ability to counteract the sharp efficient edges of contemporary kitchen design. Opt for a palette of one or two shades, and choose calming creams, soothing blues, and peaceful shades of green to create a serene effect. In addition, natural floor surfaces—stone, granite, and wood—should be kept rug-free, and pattern restricted to the occasional decorative ceramics.

PURE AND SIMPLE DETAILS

Although it is an essentially minimalist space, the Zen cooking and eating area does not lack soul. Rather, its stark decor provides a pristine arena where the addition of simple culinary items adds a grounding workaday feel. For a spontaneous Zen look, include the following: airtight Mason jars for storing dried beans, nuts, and legumes; built-in cabinets with attached plate racks for calming linear storage; pure

by sticking to simple shapes and a neutral palette, it is possible to juxtapose natural elements with contemporary designs white ceramic ware; sparkling uncut glass; simple round doorknobs, either painted or left plain; unadorned chairs; wooden bowls filled with shiny apples; and traditional silver-plated flatware.

PEACEFUL PLACE SETTINGS

In keeping with the simplicity of spiritual style, your dining area should feature a plain but elegant table as its focal point. Choose a design that has been carved from wood or stone, and make sure your chairs are made from the same material or have some link in their design to give a sense of balance and cohesion.

As far as table settings are concerned, the best way to achieve a tasteful ambience is to let the food do the talking. If your eating area is of the Zen minimalist variety, try matching a crisp white linen tablecloth with plain, upholstered chairs to create an enticingly pristine canvas. By the same token, keep your implements simple: fine bone china in white or cream, simple uncut glasses (rather than traditional stemware), and clear acrylic-resin flatware will achieve a cool and contemporary look.

To promote an organic feel in a rustic eating space, you should either leave your tabletop bare or cover it with a tablecloth made from rough-and-ready burlap. Alternatively, mark each place setting with mats made from raffia, bamboo, or cork, and furnish them with oversized wooden platters, chunky

Not only does the simplicity of the monochrome setting (below) make a dramatic statement, it also allows the diner to concentrate on the pleasure of eating and drinking, free from the encumbrance of rows of flatware and stacks of dishes.

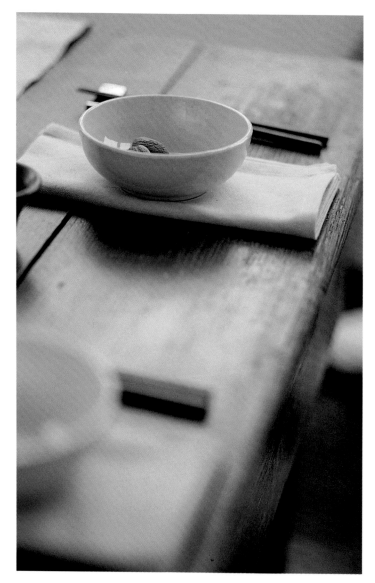

A plain but elegant table should be the main focus of your eating area (this page). Opt for a wood or stone design to help create a solid central feature, and surround it with chairs that are uniformly simple, as well as being comfortable, so your guests will want to linger over their food.

It is possible to create subtle layers of interest within your table settings through the use of pattern and texture. The mix of antique glasses and goblets (bottom) is offset by the interwoven design of the damask tablecloth, while differently patterned napkins (below) maintain a cohesive feel by sticking to the confines of a two-tone color scheme. One of the simplest and most effective ways to create a calming atmosphere in your eating space is to opt for matching table and chairs (opposite). By doing this, you can choose a more intricate design, while still maintaining an uncluttered and cohesive feel.

peasant-style pottery, bamboo-handled flatware and heavy stone candlesticks. By the same token, fussier items such as napkin rings are a definite no-no; instead, simply fold napkins in half or tie them with a length of raffia, which is as effective as it is aesthetic.

The subtle contrast of pattern, texture, and size is another important feature of table display. For example, add interest to an all-white table by laying it with a gloriously interwoven damask tablecloth—and highlight the effect with clear-glass plates. Alternatively, contrast a textured tablecloth with smooth wooden drinking cups, or ground an essentially ephemeral display by adding chunky candle blocks. It is also possible to mix patterns without the overall effect appearing too busy, as long as you stick to a simple palette of two colors. Although the tabletop should be kept simple,

decorative details still have a part to play: a pair of potted orchids, a scattering of petals, or a cluster of votive candles all promote a dreamlike quality, while a bowl of textured fruit and vegetables (such as white gourds, artichokes, and quinces) adds a sculptural look.

FEED THE BODY, NOURISH THE SOUL
Due to the evocative effect of food aromas and tastes on the psyche, the foods we prepare and serve play an important role in the atmosphere of the home. Think of the smell of freshly roasted coffee or of bread rising in the oven, or the sticky aroma of toffee, recalling childhood visits to the beach In addition, the sweet smell of chocolate has a particularly powerful effect, boosting serotonin levels in the brain before it even enters our digestive system. The spiritual kitchen is not a place of abstinence—so tuck in!

An all-white bedroom (left), complete with a huge picture window and select but functional furnishings, is perfect for those who take their sleep seriously. Add an occasional splash of neutral color to bind the look together.

Keep your sleeping space simple. Reduce furniture to the bare minimum; adopt a cohesive color scheme; and rely on space, light, and texture to create a sensory haven.

sleeping

The Zen philosophy of preserving a calm physical space in order to clear the mind is a particularly pertinent one when it comes to the spiritual bedroom. Demanding the kind of hallowed atmosphere that emanates from an inner sanctum, the ethos blends comfort with minimalism in order to boost mental and physical health.

In these days of high-stress jobs and hectic lifestyles, lack of sleep is a pressing preoccupation. Due to the ever-increasing demands of modern life, many of us are simply not clocking up enough ZZZs to keep body and soul together. But sleep is not just about quantity—it's also about quality. If our bedrooms are too hot or too cold, too cluttered or too noisy, our sleep will be seriously affected. The answer is to

keep things simple and to ban all distracting detritus from the room. The bed itself should be a island of relaxation, so prune the rest of your furniture and furnishings accordingly. Nothing should detract from the sensory delights of this room—the ultimate comfort zone of your home.

A PLACE TO DREAM
Choosing a bed is one of the most important decisions you will make when it comes to kitting out your space. Not only does a good night's sleep help restore our spirits, but creating a comfy nest is also of prime importance when you consider that we spend one third of our lives curled up under the covers. As a result, purchasing a quality mattress is key to promoting the most effective

downtime possible. Whether you choose to sleep in a romantic sleigh bed, a grand four poster, or something altogether more modern and minimal, your bed should be large enough—and luxurious enough—to spend the weekend in.

COSMIC COLOR PALETTES

White is the ideal color for the spiritual bedroom. Representing cleanliness and peace, it is also cool and contemporary, and promotes a serene sense of coherence that is conducive to relaxation. Opting for an all-white bedroom does not, however, mean you must sleep in a stark monastic cube. Instead, apply tinted paints to give your walls a warm glow; juxtapose textures and shapes to create

Far from being cold, the serene palette of the blue bedroom (above and right) is ultimately restful on the eye. The soft honey tones of the woodwork and the throw at the end of the bed provide a calming complement to the collection of similar-style pictures propped in a haphazard fashion behind the pillows.

In order to accommodate the pattern and texture of the log-cabin walls, the furnishings in the bedroom (opposite) are kept to a minimum without causing the overall effect to appear too spartan. Rather, the simple white bedlinen gives a cozy feel, while the bedside lamp adds a chic urban twist.

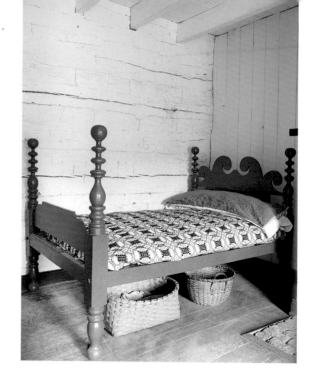

interest; and use lighting—natural and artificial—to achieve pattern and depth. A white room also provides the ideal canvas for the occasional flick of color or splash of pattern—drape a turquoise throw across snowy white sheets, for example, or top a floor lamp with a hot pink shade. Alternatively, throw a scarlet kimono across the foot of the bed, or snuggle up under a colourful antique patchwork quilt.

If white is too clinical for you, earthy neutrals in shades of buff, beige, or biscuit, or soothing shades of blue, green, yellow, gray, and pink, will also give a calming feel. Anyone suffering from insomnia should opt for blue or violet—the two most spiritual colors in the spectrum, which have been been proved to lower blood pressure and to promote peaceful feelings.

By keeping basic furnishings in the bedroom to a minimum, it is possible to introduce a bold mix of pattern and color (above). By the same token, the bare white walls and stark design of the bed (opposite, above left and below) allows for a dramatic red-and-white color scheme—from the painted woodwork, through the simple checks of the curtains, to the embroidered pattern of the antique quilts.

A mix of fabrics, in florals, stripes, and checks, on the sleigh bed (opposite, right) creates a pretty and uncontrived look in a country bedroom that is otherwise almost entirely stripped of furnishings.

One of the best ways to enhance light and space in the bedroom is to opt for a cheerful color scheme. The yellow and white palette in the space (left) is a perfect example of this, helping to open out the room and prevent the patchwork quilt and drawer-lined wall from appearing too busy.

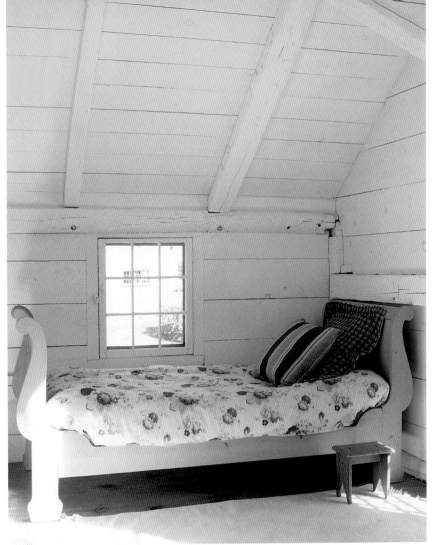

think of your bed as a remote island floating in a calm sea

TURN ON, CHILL OUT

Because it has such a strong impact on mood, it is important to get the lighting of your bedroom just right. Natural light nourishes our souls, while the artificial illuminations that supplement it, such as the gentle glow from a bedside lamp, should help you to unwind. If possible, try to make the room you sleep in faces east. This way you will benefit from the galvanizing energy of the morning sun, which provides the necessary impetus to get out of bed. That said, a harsh glare

choose air and water colors in muted shades to soothe the soul

A stainless-steel trolley, pink curtains, and Moroccan slippers in the bedroom (above) create a lighthearted quirky feel, although the overall ambience is a restful one.

The regimental decor and neutral palette in the sleeping space (left) is prevented from becoming too impersonal by the floaty pink drapes at the window and the spray of flowers on the bedside table.

The grandeur of the carved bed (opposite) is complemented by a pair of navy lampshades, while the soft woolen throws are soothing against the coarse canework of the bed frame.

The intricate design of the wrought-iron bed (below) is calm and serene, thanks to its elegant proportions and the plain bedlinen. The spindly legs of the furnishings—which seem to float above the floor— are countered by the bare wooden boards.

can be invasive, so opt for blinds or curtains made from light-filtering fabrics such as voile. An advantage of floaty drapes is their ability to emphasize the movement of air, which will also help to enhance a spiritually ephemeral feel.

Artificial lighting should be soft and relaxing. Mix ambient illuminations and specific task lights (essential for reading), in order to create an intimate glow that is conducive to sleep. In addition, make sure your light levels are adjustable, because hard bright light in a minimalist space can make it seem cold and clinical. Instead, opt for indirect lighting that has a two-tone effect—creating pools of warmth on walls and ceilings, while leaving other areas mysteriously shadowy.

UNASHAMEDLY LUXURIOUS FABRICS
Although the spiritual bedroom is fundamentally minimalist in style, it is in no way austere. Choose linens and silks to usher in a mood of sensuality, and make your bed a key site for the creation of a simply sybaritic style.

We all know the feeling of bliss that comes from climbing into bed between fresh sheets that have been aired and scented. The sensation of natural fabrics on your bare skin is one of the best soul-soothers in the world, while falling back on freshly plumped pillows helps to ease away stresses and strains of the day. As a result, it is vitally important that your bedlinen is made from high-quality, natural fibers. (It

A combination of pink and white creates a calming color scheme (opposite), while the dark metal spindles of the headboard help to anchor the look and prevent it from appearing too ephemeral.

The slippery sheen of the bedcover (left) contrasts with the stark lines of the bench, slatted chair, and gooseneck lamp, in order to create a pleasing balance between luxury and rigor.

choose sheets in calming colors, and contrast textures and styles to prevent your sleeping space from appearing too bland

Semi-opaque glass bricks, lilac walls, and a beechwood Bunny chair lift the monastic-looking bedroom (left) out of the ordinary and give it a funky twist.

The cream-painted paneling and bed (above) create a cozy reassuring feel, while the crisp cotton pillows and plain bedside table complete the look, which is fresh and inviting.

goes without saying that the spiritual bedroom is a pure-cotton, rather than a cotton-blend kind of place.)

If your sleeping area is a symphony in white, then pristine bedlinen is a must. Thankfully, there are numerous different styles of plain bed dressings on the market, allowing for the creation of interest within the confines of a minimalist palette. For example, contrast stark white sheets with a sumptuous satin comforter, or combine delicately detailed fabrics such as lace and eyelet with more robust ones like pique or wool. A dove-white bed can also be enhanced by the addition of floaty drapes falling from a corona attached to the ceiling. This way, you can turn your bed into a seductive haven of dreams and romance.

Bedrooms decorated in neutral colors also provide a variety of options in terms of tactile choice. Organic

Far from being gray and depressing, the sophisticated color scheme in the bedroom (opposite) provides a calming antidote to the chaos of color and clutter of the outside world; instead, the look is crisp and light.

A scatter of cushions is one of the quickest ways to soften the stark minimalism of an all-white bedroom (left). Here, the simple color scheme of brown and white allows for the introduction of different patterns and textures, without creating a conflict of interest.

A raw linen pillow cover (below) has a pleasing texture, its coarse fibers contrasting with its soft functionalism.

materials such as alpaca, burlap, and linen tone well with wooden beds, while a warm mix of luxurious textures helps to promote a reassuring grounded feel. Take your pick from brushed cotton, cashmere, suede, angora, or mohair.

SLEEPY SCENTS

Said to promote physical, mental, and spiritual wellbeing, lavender is one of the best known cures for insomnia. Administer it by spritzing your sheets with lavender water or by putting a couple of drops of essential oil onto your pillow. If symptoms persist, step up your campaign by slipping a lavender bag in your pillowcase, and keep a bowl of dried lavender on your bedside table.

The best way to create a peaceful washing space is to keep the fixtures in your bathroom simple. Faucets should be plumbed into the wall (opposite) to keep bathtub and basin edges clear, while industrial building materials such as concrete and glass (left) offer an attractive and durable alternative in the bathroom.

bathing

Since the 1950s, the bathroom has metamorphosed from a washing space into a haven of relaxation and pampering.

The development of the bathroom from a functional place of ablutions reflects a growing interest in our mental and spiritual health, and takes its cue from traditional Japanese bath-house design, which focuses on water therapy as an effective way to soothe the soul. As a result, Western bathrooms are becoming increasingly like spas in order to recreate a similarly serene feel. Fixtures blend seamlessly with the overall decor; color is reduced to one or two shades; and ugly pipes are boxed away. This way, we can concentrate on the ritual of purification without becoming distracted by visual detritus.

CLEANSE THE SPACE, PURIFY THE SOUL
Keeping your bathroom simple demands the adoption of a strict minimalist code. Plumb faucets into a facing wall so that bathtub and basin edges remain

111

clear, and replace cosmetic-laden shelves with unobtrusive cabinets. Decorative accessories, too, should be kept to a minimum: a single picture or potted palm may be enough if spiritual rejuvenation is your main aim. If you feel the need for a greater display of personal accessories in your bathing space, stick to natural objects, focusing on textural contrast rather than harsh colors.

SLEEK SURFACE TREATMENTS

Although the spiritual bathroom is an essentially minimalist space, this does not mean there is a lack of choice when it comes to surface treatments. Rather, there are myriad finishes available—from smooth ceramics to gleaming stainless steel, patterned marbles to cool glass, and warm woods to tinted concrete.

With today's emphasis on water therapy as an effective salve for the soul, bathrooms (opposite) are becoming increasingly minimalist, taking inspiration from modern spas. Colors are clean and cool, and furnishings and fixtures pruned to the bare essentials.

A softer feel can be created with the use of warm colors and interesting textures (above); likewise, a display of crystals is decorative without appearing overly fussy (above left).

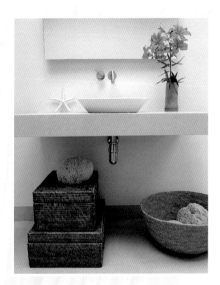

Although it is pared down, the washing space (opposite and left) **has a warm earthy feel, thanks to a rattan storage selection and the soft circle of the stone basin. A couple of sea sponges and a simple vase of flowers complete the organic look.**

shades of white or cream provide a pristine backdrop in which to cleanse body and soul

Whether you choose a boxy Japanese-style tub or an antique roll-top one (below), **your bathtub should be long enough and deep enough for a seriously good wallow—a place where you can read, meditate, or enjoy a calming cup of herbal tea.**

If your washing space has an earthy organic theme, then a soft wooden finish is advised. Not only does wood look great against a backdrop of calming neutrals, but if you choose a hardwearing variety that has been treated to resist water, you can also use it for fixtures such as your bathtub, basin, and toilet. Favored by the Japanese for hundreds of years, a wooden tub offers a wonderfully elemental bathing experience—combining a warm tactile feel with the fabulous aroma of wood that is released when your tub fills with hot water.

Stone is another effective treatment in the bathroom, providing a feeling of immutability that contrasts with the edgy hi-tech world outside. Like wood, stone is tough, durable, and water-resistant. It is also available in a wide variety of types and finishes: choose granite if you want to create a macho urban feel or soft sandstone for a warmer, earthier look. It is also possible to opt for super-deluxe marble—this once impossibly expensive stone is now more cheaply available in the form of tiles, veneers, and marble-and-resin composites. Alternatively, opt for

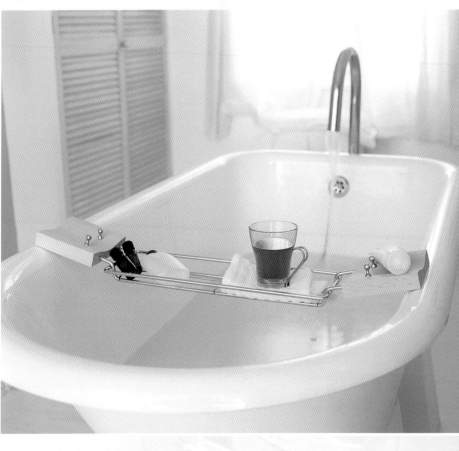

cast concrete, which is now as popular indoors as it is out. Mixed according to a number of specialized finishes, concrete can match much of the sensual appeal of stone—its texture and color manipulated to produce a variety of pleasing results.

SIMPLE SHADES

One of the best ways to create a cleansing ambience in the bathroom is to keep your palette to a minimum of one or two colors. It doesn't matter what shades you choose as long as they are clear and tonal (strong, dense colors are likely to restrain, rather than free, the spirit). Shades of white or cream are ideal, providing a clear, light feel—unlike the old-fashioned dark-colored sanitaryware, which has fallen from grace.

This watery room is the perfect place to mix reflective surfaces. The smoked-glass shelf, shiny basin, and chrome fixtures (left) fit the bill nicely, and contrast with the fissured strata of the limestone wall tiles.

Expensive designer lotions and potions have no place in the peaceful bathing space. Instead, the look is natural and organic, relying on simple soaps and plain cotton towels (above) for maximum effect.

The soft sandstone of the bathroom (opposite) creates a warm earthy feel, while the niche position of the tub compounds the sense of sanctuary.

Thanks to its associations with the sea and sky, blue also works well in the spiritual bathroom. Light variations of this watery shade will help to calm the body and still the mind. In addition, blue provides the perfect complement to white, while the combination of these two colors gives an appropriate seaside feel and prevents your space from appearing too clinical.

For a calming back-to-basics look that is more homey than spalike, choose a neutral palette in muted earth colors. Soft greens, pale browns, and sandy yellows all give a natural grounded effect, as well as providing the perfect complement to surfaces such as stone and wood. In addition, a neutral palette provides the ideal backdrop for the addition of organic accessories such as sisal baskets, loofahs, seashells, and natural sponges.

CALM REFLECTIONS

The elemental aspect of bathing means that light is an important aspect in the bathroom, helping to compound our connection with the natural world. As a result, many modern bathrooms are designed to harness as much light as possible—either through the addition of extra windows or via a skylight positioned directly above your washing area. This way, bathers can enjoy the great outdoors through the contemplation of clouds, treetops, and birds in flight as they lie back in the tub.

If your wash space is the pristine all-white variety, reinforced glass is the ideal complement, helping to imbue the space with a light, ephemeral feel. Glass

A gray-brown limestone, mottled with fossil remains, is saved from being overly cool and dark (left) by the warm-toned slatted blinds and the wall length of mirrored cabinets, which help bounce light back into the room. Further contrast is provided by the vertical ribbing cut into the bathtub surround and walls.

Reflective surfaces such as chrome and shiny ceramics (above and right) are another way to make your bathroom appear lighter and brighter, especially if your chosen color scheme revolves around dark and dramatic stone.

is extremely versatile, durable, and easy to clean, as well as being available in a variety of forms—including plain, opaque, colored, and frosted. Use it for walls, doors, and screens, or in the construction of a shower cubicle, basin, or bathtub.

It is also possible to make your bathroom appear bigger and brighter through the use of artfully placed mirrors, which bounce light back into the room. In addition, reflective glass can be used to create alternative dimensions, offering bathers the magical sensation of wallowing in an illusory space.

SOOTHING LOTIONS, POTIONS, AND ACCESSORIES

In a truly peaceful bathing space, cosmetic items should be hidden from sight. Evidence of the mundane essentials needed to keep body and soul together will destroy the soothing ambience of the room, so make sure toothpaste, razors, and cotton balls are neatly stowed in a streamlined cabinet.

Attaining a truly peaceful bathroom demands a strict code: fixtures should blend seamlessly with the overall decor; color should be limited to one or two shades; and the visual distraction of decorative elements kept to a minimum.

A series of identically placed windows and carefully positioned mirrors provide a soothing sense of continuity in the washing space (far left and left), connecting bathtub, basin, and shower cubicle with total fluidity. In addition, their circular shape creates a calming antidote to the rigid lines of the wall tiles.

A shiny rubber floor and long elegant bathtub give the washing space (below) an almost monastic appearance.

a pristine space allows you to concentrate all your attention on the ritual of purification

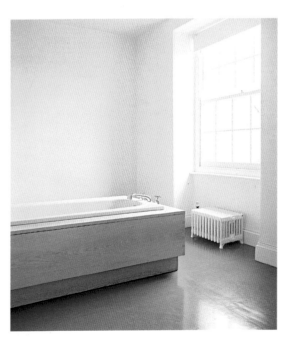

It is acceptable, however, to display a few essential unguents. Decant shampoo, conditioner, shower gel, and bath oils into spiritually aesthetic bottles, and make a display of organic soap, sea sponges, and loofahs—all of which add an earthy, elemental feel. Plants also work well in the spiritual bathroom, absorbing extra humidity and making your space feel fresh and alive. The occasional frondy fern will help to soften hard angular surfaces, while plants with scented flowers will add a delicate fragrance—orchids are a particular favorite, since they thrive in a humid atmosphere and add an exotic, mystical feel.

The customized Eames chair and velvet pillow are a far cry from the dull uniformity of office furniture, while tin cans, which have been stripped of their labels, add a dash of fashionable eco-chic.

Whether you plan to work from home fulltime, or simply want to create an "admin" area where you can write letters and catch up on paperwork, it is vital that you create an organized space in which to focus the mind.

working

In the space of a single generation, communications technology has revolutionized our working lives. Thanks to the advent of email and the Internet, we can now dispatch the printed word at the touch of a button, glean information on any given subject in minutes, and communicate with people on the other side of the world at a fraction of the cost of a telephone call. As a result, an increasing number of people are working from home—relying on computer technology to keep them in touch with the outside world. This arrangement is particularly effective for those seeking a peaceful working environment in which to nurture mind, body, and soul. In addition, working from home offers an escape route from the irritations of office life, where ringing phones, harassed colleagues, endless meetings, and the daily commute all fray our nerves and deplete our spiritual reserves.

ORGANIZING YOUR WORK ETHICS

Your workspace should be designed to cater for the work you want to achieve—be it negotiating a complex business deal, writing a book, designing a Web site, or simply sorting out your accounts. Without doubt, you will perform much more efficiently if you have a well-ordered, comfortable, and visually appealing place to do this in.

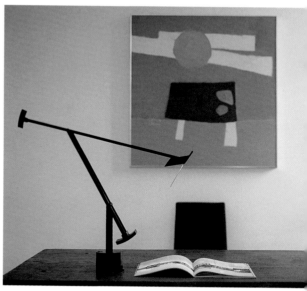

It is also important that you invest time and money in the creation of a conducive working environment, as any initial outlay will quickly be repaid in terms of increased productivity. As a result, consider the conversion potential of any spare space in your home—the attic, a roomy walk-in closet or the conservatory, for example. Alternatively, build a workstation into the corner of an underused room, such as a dining room or spare bedroom.

DIVINE DECOR INSPIRATION

One of the best aspects of working from home is the exhilarating liberation from standard office furnishings. While elephant-gray desks, brooding computers, and institutionalized carpeting are a fact of life in offices

It is not necessary to set aside a whole room in order to create an effective work area. Instead, the cleverly compact office unit (left) tucks neatly into a corner and incorporates enough space for a computer, printer, and fax without appearing overbearing. In addition, its light, bright, and uplifting color scheme is conducive to creativity.

Although starkly minimalist in appearance, a good deal of thought has gone into the design of the office (opposite, right)—from the practicality of the cantilevered adjustable desk lamp designed by Richard Sapper to the solidity of the old wooden desk. The result is an effective workspace that is both comfortable and aesthetic.

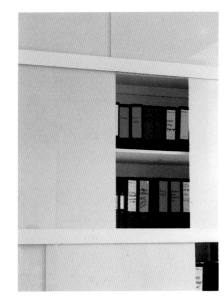

a pale and interesting palette creates the perfect environment for a productive outlay

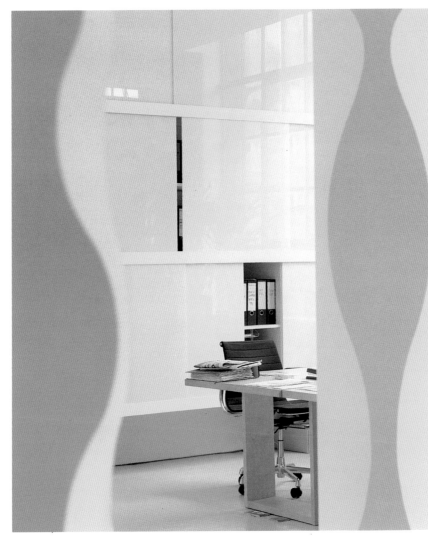

across the world, the home office is a much more aesthetic affair, designed to reflect the personality of its occupant and effect first-rate results.

The most effective workspace is simple but slick— relying on a handful of furnishings for an uncluttered environment where ideas can flow freely. Once again, a pale palette is best for promoting clarity of thought, with neutrals such as stone, ivory, and string coming top of the class for creating a contemplative feel. Alternatively, opt for clear tones such as duck's egg blue or primrose yellow, against which a modern print or a jewel-bright chair will create an inspiring focal point.

Good lighting is also important in the home office. If possible, place your workstation near a window, as natural light aids creativity. As far as artificial illumination is concerned, make sure a gooseneck lamp is an integral feature of your desk.

If your work creates volumes of paperwork, a wall of built-in units (above and left) will provide ample storage space. Make sure your cabinets are big enough to accommodate bulky box files.

A bright-red chair adds a cheerful note to the simple workstation (opposite), while the natural light that streams through the big window imbues the businesslike environment with an upbeat positive feel.

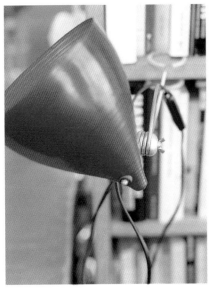

A smattering of funky additions creates a personalized charm which, in turn, aids creativity. A black-and-white photograph, vase, and modern floor light (above) soften the hard lines of the industrial workspace, as well as helping to counter the harsh urban view.

The furnishings for a home office should be chosen carefully. Good-quality, sturdy storage solutions (above left) will repay you in years of service. Make sure, too, that your workstation is always properly illuminated—adjustable lamps are ideal (left).

SITTING PRETTY

Your desk and chair are the most important purchases you will make when setting up a home office. Even if your budget is limited, it is vital that you spend time and money sourcing the best ergonomic designs available, because they will protect against debilitating conditions such as low back pain and repetitive strain injury.

Start off by choosing a desk that is large enough to accommodate your computer, mouse mat, phone, and in-tray, without cramping your style. If your work demands creativity, source a round desk that will encourage original thoughts and ideas. By contrast, if your business involves working with numbers, a conventional rectangular or square desk is a better choice.

As far as chairs are concerned, choose an adjustable style that will provide good lower back support—this is vital if you intend to spend long periods sitting at your desk. Chairs on castors are another good idea, since they allow for flexible movement around the work area.

POSITIVE VIBES AND STIMULATING SCENTS

To work at peak efficiency, you need a stimulating atmosphere. One of the best ways to achieve this is by investing in an ionizer to combat toxic computer emissions. Add a couple of leafy plants, also known for their air-purifying abilities, to compound the effect.

Aromatherapy is another way of providing an invigorating work environment. The following fragrances are known for their mind-enhancing properties: for clarity of thought, choose rosemary or basil; to counteract mental fatigue, basil; to stimulate the brain, eucalyptus or sage; to boost memory, ginger, basil, lemon, grapefruit, rosemary, cilantro, or peppermint; and for creative inspiration, frankincense, bergamot, rose, jasmine, or cinnamon.

wooden furnishings in the workspace symbolize growth and development

One of the perks of working from home is liberation from grungey office furnishings. The simple wooden trestle table (above left) creates ample space for catching up on paperwork, while the gingham-covered chair gives a cheerful lift. In addition, a white-painted filing cabinet blends seamlessly into the space, while the aroma from the pot of rosemary helps to promote clarity of thought.

If you suffer from lack of concentration, light a candle (far left). Not only will the flame provide a calming focal point, but the scent of aromatherapy candles can also help to kickstart the brain. Flowers and herbs are similarly stimulating (left); choose mint as a powerful aid to concentration.

It is not necessary to opt for a standard desk and chair in order to create an effective workspace. As long as your chair is at the right height for your desk, it is possible to choose a variety of different furnishing styles. A café chair combined with an old sewing-machine table (this page) provides a good set up for writing the odd letter, while a comfy armchair is ideal for flicking through magazines.

A glass wall overlooking a calm expanse of water creates a peaceful vista for the occupants of this house. Not only does the seamless transition between outside and in provide a connection with nature, but the reflective quality of the water is also meditative and restful.

outdoor living

You needn't live in a country retreat with big sweeping lawns in order to create a tranquil space where you can touch the earth and feel the air.

In the same way that plants wither and die from lack of light, so the human psyche shrivels when it is deprived of contact with the rhythms of the earth. As a result, it is vital that our environments include an area where we can benefit from the healing power of nature.

It doesn't matter whether your exterior space consists of a vast rambling garden or a concrete balcony the size of a handkerchief—or even if you have no outdoor space at all. What is important is that you create a tranquil retreat where you can reconnect with mother earth. By committing yourself to the loving maintenance of your garden—or to bringing the outdoors into your home—you will create the optimum conditions for your spirituality to flourish and grow.

BLURRING THE BOUNDARIES

The importance of connecting with the natural world cannot be over-emphasized in the home. Even if you have a generous-sized backyard, it is still necessary to establish a link between your interior space and your exterior one. The best way to blur the boundaries is to install floor-to-ceiling sliding glass doors and to maintain the same

THE SPACE outdoor living

The calming space of the bedroom (right) has
been enhanced by the simple balcony accessed
through French doors. Not only does this provide
increased light and space, but the view of sky
and treetops is supremely restorative.

An indoor pond has been created amid the stone
and concrete confines of a converted warehouse
(below). The design is based on the peaceful
premise of a Zen garden, including the addition of
a large boulder as part of the pond wall. However,
the contemporary setting gives a quirky twist and
yanks the look into the twenty-first century.

Converted from a former dairy barn, the elegant
lap pool (opposite) has been painted bright white
to resemble a boathouse. The collection of
floating balls increases the feeling of tranquillity
and reflection.

by creating a seamless transition between inside and out, you compound the sense of calm continuity in your home

floor surface on each side. If you have no outside space whatsoever, it does not
mean you need to feel isolated from nature. Instead, combine elements such as
skylights, plants, and water features to create an indoor "garden."

CREATING A ZEN GARDEN OF NATURAL HARMONY
One of the most effective ways to "spiritualize" an outside space is to imitate
the Zen gardens of old and to arrange stones, shrubs, water, trees, and sand to
create an energizing balance of yin and yang. However, it is not necessary to adhere
to a rigorous Japanese design in order to create a tranquil space. As long as clutter
is kept to a minimum and natural materials are used, it is possible to promote
feelings of serenity through the addition of a few key features. For example, if you
have a small backyard, use silvery wooden decking, gravel, or simple flagstones to
create a calming, grounded feel. Alternatively, pave your space with tinted concrete

Even if your outside area is the size of a handkerchief, it is possible to create a natural haven by dint of lateral thinking. The wooden slatted screen (opposite) creates an ordered sense of Zen tranquillity, while the lush foliage overhanging it softens the look. By the same token, the plain bench running alongside provides conducive seating, thanks to the welcoming addition of a single pillow.

A tiny city roof terrace (left)—with the addition of wooden decking, a couple of comfortable wicker chairs, and a selection of cheerful tubs and fragrant plantings—is all it takes to commune with the natural world.

If you have no access to an outside space, it is still perfectly possible to create a similar feel indoors. The generous-sized skylight, flagstone floor, and foliage-filled hanging basket (above) give a natural airy look.

and add wispy ornamental grasses to soften the effect. It is also possible to make your outside space more peaceful through the addition of furniture and accessories in calming shapes and interesting textures. For instance, a trio of different-sized stone balls will create a soothing focal point, while a simple wood bench (preferably placed in the shade of an ancient tree) presents the perfect meditation spot. Cane or bamboo chairs also compound the elemental look, as do portable lanterns in hammered steel.

GO GREEN WITH NON-FLOWERING PLANTS

Although aroma is a key feature in the home, the presence of fragrant flowers is not integral to the creation of a soulful outside space. Instead, tall grasses and leafy plants take center stage by emphasizing the all-green cohesion and calm of Zen garden design.

In addition to being fashionable, wispy greenery is also gratifyingly easy to care for. Choose from fast-growing golden or black bamboo—

movement induce spiritual calm, but the appearance of running water also frees our creativity and helps us to think more spontaneously. In Zen philosophy, it is thought to carry chi—the energizing force essential for life. By contrast, still water is quiet, tranquil, and serene; its reflective qualities help to expand our horizons, while its glassy depths aid meditation. If you have a pond, enhance spiritual feelings by adding water lilies—which represent purity and decency according to Zen beliefs—and fish, which the dictates of feng shui say will auger health and prosperity.

If your outside space is limited to a small area, create a mini water feature by covering the base of a large glass bowl or vase with pebbles and filling it with water. Float a flower head or candle on the surface, to highlight the soothing ripples produced by natural air currents.

Vital for inducing feelings of tranquillity, water is a key feature in the creation of a peaceful outside space. Whether you opt for the mellifluous sound of water falling from a spout (left), **or the meditative depths of a still-water pond, is up to you.**

An outside wash space (below right) **is a perfect way to allow everyday activities to spill outdoors in good weather.**

A wooden deck (opposite) **large enough for a table and chairs is the ideal way to enjoy the outdoors. Choose natural materials and simple furnishings that will blend harmoniously with the surrounding environs.**

which introduces movement and height—or the swaying grace of ornamental grasses, which quiver even in the lightest of breezes. Alternatively, if you want a graphic look, fill smooth silver planters with succulents and surround them with artful pebble arrangements. Pots of blue-green *Helictotrichon* grass also work well, promoting feelings of vibrancy and health, while the feathery foliage of silver- and gray-leafed plants introduces a subtle color contrast.

WATER, STAFF OF LIFE

Known for its remedial properties, the cleansing essence of water has been used in religious practices for thousands of years. Accordingly, water helps to still our minds and allow our thoughts to ascend to a higher plane. Introduce water to your outside area through the addition of a spouting fountain or a glassy pond—both are highly effective ways to quieten the mind and promote feelings of reflection. Moving water is dynamic, vibrant, and alive. Not only does its lyrical

sources

Key: a=above, b=below, l=left,
r=right, c=center

Artemide GB Ltd
323 City Road
London EC1V 1LJ, UK
Tel: +44 20 7833 1755
*Acclaimed Italian design company
responsible for many modern
lighting classics*

Atrium
Centrepoint
22–24 St Giles High Street
London WC2H 8LN, UK
Tel: +44 20 7379 7288
*The very latest lighting and
furniture from renowned
contemporary designers as well as
many modern lighting classics*

Carden Cunietti
83 Westbourne Park Road
London W2 5QH, UK
*Interior-design shop mixing old
and new*

Farrow & Ball
Uddens Estate
Wimbourne
Dorset BH21 7NL, UK
Paint

Intérieurs
Tel: 212 343 0800
*Asian-inspired furniture as well as
19th- and 20th-century antiques*

SKK
34 Lexington Street
London W1R 3HR, UK
Tel: +44 20 7434 4095
*Architectural lighting consultancy
and stockist of cutting-edge
young lighting designers*

Story
Tel: +44 20 7377 6377
*Appointment only
Personal selection of old and new
furniture and accessories*

Tsé Tsé at Galerie Sentou
26 boulevard Raspail
75007 Paris, France
Tel: +33 1 45 49 00 05
and at Maryse Boxer Design
26 Sloane Street
London SW1X 7QL
Tel: +44 20 7 245 9493
*Elegant, quirky lighting designs by
a stylish young French company*

ARCHITECTS AND DESIGNERS
WHOSE WORK HAS BEEN
FEATURED IN THIS BOOK:

Asfour Guzy
594 Broadway, Suite 1204
New York NY 10012
Tel: 212 334 9350
Fax: 212 334 9009
Page 17

Ash Sakula Architects
38 Mount Pleasant
London WC1X 0AN, UK
Pages 79, 89

Azman Owens
Architects
8 St Albans Place
London NW1 0NX, UK
Tel: +44 20 7354 2955
Fax: +44 20 7354 2966
Page 78l&r

Babylon Design Ltd
Lighting Designers
301 Fulham Road
London SW10 9QH, UK
Tel: +44 20 7376 7233
Email:
info@babylondesign.demon.co.uk
*Lights by up-and-coming
designers such as Peter Wylly,
Ross Menuez, and Roland
Simmons*
Pages 22, 124r, 125, 127r

Barefoot Elegance
Dot Spikings & Jennifer Castle
3537 Old Conejo Road, Suite 105
Newbury Park CA 91320
Tel: 805 499 5959
Pages 12, 13, 30, 33r, 38r, 43

JoAnn Barwick
Interior Designer
P.O. Box 982
Boca Grande FL 33921
Pages 83br, 103r

Claire Bataille & Paul ibens
Design NV
Architects
Vekestratt 13 Bus 14
2000 Antwerp
Belgium
Tel: +32 3 231 3593
Fax: +32 3 213 8639
Pages 81, 118–119, 119b

Bedmar & Shi Designers Pte Ltd
12a Keong Saik Road
Singapore 089119
Tel: +65 22 77117
Fax: +65 22 77695
*Singapore-based firm established
in 1980 specializing in residential
projects and also in interior design
mainly for restaurants and offices*
Pages 97, 136a

**Laura Bohn Design Associates,
Inc.**
30 West 26th Street
New York NY 10010
Tel: 212 645 3636
Fax: 212 645 3639
Page 135r

Bowles & Linares
32 Hereford Road
London W2 5AJ, UK
Tel: +44 20 7229 9886
Page 92r

Ann Boyd Design Ltd
33 Elystan Street
London SW3 3NT, UK
Tel: +44 20 7591 0202
Fax: +44 20 7591 0404
Page 40a

Nancy Braithwaite Interiors
2300 Peachtree Road, Suite C101
Atlanta GA 30309
Pages 18, 50r

Cabot Design Ltd
Interior Design
1925 Seventh Avenue, Suite 71
New York NY 10026
Tel: 212 222 9488
Email: eocabot@aol.com
Page 55

Circus Architects
Unit 1, Summer Street
London EC1R 5BD, UK
Tel: +44 20 7833 1999
Page 90

Conner Prairie Museum
134000 Alisonville Road
Fishers IN 46038
Pages 11,102a

Damien D'Arcy Associates
9 Lamington Street
London W6 0HU, UK
Tel: +44 20 8741 1193
Fax: +44 20 8563 7784
Page 113

**De Le Cuona Textile and Home
Collection**
9–10 Osborne Mews
Windsor SL4 3DE, UK
Tel: +44 1753 830301
email: bernie@softech.co.uk
www.delecuona.co.uk
Please call for stockists
Pages 62, 63l

De Metz Architects
Unit 4, 250 Finchley Road
London NW3 6DN, UK
Tel: +44 20 7435 1144
Page 23

Terry Dorrough Architect
14 Riverview Avenue
Dangar Island NSW 2083
Austrailia
Tel: +61 2 9985 7729
Fax: +61 2 9985 7177
*Design of houses and small
projects*
Page 134

Robert Dye Associates
68–74 Rochester Place
London NW1 9JX, UK
Tel: +44 20 7267 9388
Fax: +44 20 7267 5963
Page 100

Jamie Falla
MooArc
198 Blackstock Road
London N5 1EN, UK
Tel: +44 20 7345 1729
Page 53l

Han Feng
Fashion Designer
333 West 39th Street, 12th Floor
New York NY 10018
Tel: 212 695 9509
Page 61

Ken Foreman
Architect
105 Duane Street
New York NY 10007
Tel/Fax: 212 924 4503
Page 112r

Belmont Freeman Architects
Project Team: Belmont Freeman
(Principal Designer), Alane Truitt
Sangho Park
110 West 40th Street
New York NY 10018
Tel: 212 382 3311
Fax: 212 730 1229
Page 126

Zina Glazebrook
ZG Design
10 Wireless Road
East Hampton NY 11937
Tel: 631 329 7486
Fax: 631 329 2087
Email: dzina@ATT.net
www.zgdesign.com
Pages 24, 133

Glomdalsmueet
Museum for Østerdalen and Solar
2400 Elverum, Norway
Page 57l

Mark Guard Architects
161 Whitfield Street
London W1P 5RY, UK
Tel: +44 20 7380 1199
Pages 98–99

Alastair Hendy
*Food Writer, Art Director and
Designer*
Fax: +44 20 7739 6040
Pages 2, 8–9, 60

John C. Hope Architects
3 St Bernard's Crescent
Edinburgh EH4 1NR, UK
Tel: +44 131 315 2215
Fax: +44 131 315 2911
Page 15

Hudson Featherstone
Rowland Hill House
49–59 Old Street
London EC1V 9HX, UK
Tel: +44 20 7490 5656
Page 121b

Jacomini Interior Design
1701 Brun, Suite 101
Houston TX 77019
Pages 83 al, 103al&bl

Joanna Jefferson Architects
222 Oving Road
Chichester
West Sussex PO19 4EJ, UK
Tel: +44 1243 532398
Fax: +44 1243 531 550
Email: jjeffearch@aol.com
Pages 70–71

Just Design Ltd
80 Fifth Avenue, 18th Floor
New York NY 10011
Tel: 212 243 6544
Fax: 212 229 1112
Email: wbp@angel.net
Page 25

Kayode Lipede
Tel: +44 20 7794 7535
Page 90

James Lynch, D.A.D. Associates
112–116 Old Street
London EC1V 9BG, UK
Page 36

Ocke Mannerfelf
Architect
Hamnvägen 8
S-18351 Täby, Sweden
Pages 50–51

Mary MacCarthy
Decorative paintwork and murals
Tel: +44 1328 730133
Pages 67bl

Hilton McConnico
Interior Home Designer
8 rue Antoine Panier
93170 Bagnolet, France
Tel: +33 1 43 62 53 16
Fax: +33 1 43 62 73 44
Email: hmc@club-internet.fr
Page 121al&ar

David Mikhail Architects
68–74 Rochester Place
London NW1 9JX, UK
Tel: +44 20 7485 4696
Fax: +44 20 7267 8661
www.dmikhail.freeserve.co.uk
Page 119a

L.A. Morgan
Interior Designer
P.O. Box 39
Hadlyme CT 06439
Tel: 860 434 0304
Fax: 860 434 3103
Page 42r

Mullman Seidman Architects
Architecture and Interior Design
443 Greenwich Street
New York NY 10013
Tel: 212 431 0770
Fax: 212 431 8428
Email: mullseid@monmouth.com
Page 54r

Roger Oates Design
Shop & Showroom:
1 Munro Terrace
Off Cheyne Walk
Chelsea
London SW10 0DL, UK
Studio Shop:
The Long Barn
Eastnor, Ledbury
Herefordshire HR8 1EL, UK
Tel: +44 1531 631611
Rugs and runners. Call for mail-order catalogue
Pages 16, 58c, 58r, 104l

Orefelt Associates
Design Team: Gunner Orefelt, John
Massey, Gianni Botsford, Jason
Griffiths
4 Portobello Studios
5 Hayden's Place
London W11 1LY, UK
Tel: +44 20 7243 3181
Fax: +44 20 7792 1126
Email: orefelt@msn.com
Pages 110, 111

Graham Phillips RIBA
Architect
Pages 3, 130–131

Mathew Priestman Architects
6–8 Emerald Street
London WC1N 3QA, UK
Tel: +44 20 7404 3113
Front jacket

Potted Gardens
27 Bedford Street
New York NY 10014
Page 82

Lena Proudlock
Denim in Style
Drews House
Leighterton
Gloucestershire GL8 8UN, UK
Tel/Fax: +44 1666 890230
Page 20

Reed Creative Services Ltd
151a Sydney Street
London SW3 6NT, UK
Tel: +44 20 7565 0066
Page 29bl

Les Reedman
Chartered Architect and
Architectural Historian
PO Box 148
Brooklyn NSW 2083
Australia
Tel: +61 2 9985 7893
Fax: (Brooklyn P.O.)
+61 2 9985 7658
Page 137

Nico Rensch Architeam
Tel: +44 411 412898
Page 109l

Johanne Riss
*Stylist, Designer and Fashion
Designer*
35 Place du Nouveau Marché aux
Graens
1000 Brussels, Belgium
Tel: +32 2 513 0900
Fax: +32 2 514 3284
Page 132l

Jim Ruscitto
Architect
Ruscitto, Latham, Blanton
PO Box 419
Sun Valley ID 83353
Pages 48, 57c, 101

SCDA Architects
10 Teck Lim Road
Singapore 088386
Tel: +65 324 5458
Fax: +65 324 5450
Email: scda@cyberway.com.sg
Page 116l

Johnson Schwinghammer
339 West 38th Street, #9
New York NY 10018
Tel: 212 643 1552
Pages 3al, 29al, 75

Sheila Scoles
Designer
Tel: +44 1480 498241
Page 84al

Sequana
64 avenue de la Motte Picquet
75015 Paris, France
Tel: +33 1 45 66 58 40
Fax: +33 1 45 67 99 81
Email: sequana@wandoo.fr
Page 64l

Shelton, Mindel & Associates
216 West 18th Street
New York NY 10011
Tel: 212 243 3939
Pages 3al, 29al, 75

Ann Shore
Tel/Fax: +44 20 7377 6377
*Appointment only
London-based designer and stylist,
and owner of Story
Personal selection of old and new
furniture and accessories.*
Pages 39r, 49, 65, 128bl, 135l

Square Foot Properties Ltd
50 Britton Street
London EC1M 5UP, UK
Tel: +44 20 7253 2527
Fax: +44 20 7253 2528
Page 107bl

Guy Stansfeld
Tel: +44 20 7727 0133
Pages 14br, 112l

Seth Stein
15 Grand Union Centre
West Row
Ladbroke Grove
London W10 5AS, UK
Tel: +44 20 8968 8581
Page 95

Stickland Coombe Architecture
258 Lavender Hill
London SW11 1LJ, UK
Tel: +44 20 7924 1699
Fax: +44 20 7652 1788
Email:
nick@scadesign.freeserve.co.uk
Pages 108, 120

Sally Storey
John Cullen Lighting
585 King's Road
London SW6 2EH, UK
Tel: +44 20 7371 5400
Page 29bl

**Stutchbury & Pape Architecture +
Landscape Architecture**
4/364 Barrenjoey Road
Newport NSW 2106
Austrailia
Tel: +61 2 9979 5030
Fax: +61 2 9979 5367
Email: snpala@ozemail.com.au
*Have a reputation for innovative
thinking and environmental
sensitivity. The land, the site, and
place are seen as directives toward
the solution of formulating a building*
Page 132a

Bruno Tanquerel
Artist
2 Passage St Sébastien
75011 Paris, France
Tel: +33 1 43 57 03 93
Page 117

Touch Interior Design
Tel: +44 20 7498 6409
Page 37

Urban Research Laboratory
3 Plantain Place
Crosby Row
London SE1 1YN, UK
Tel: +44 20 7403 2929
Email: jeff@urbanresearchlab.com
Page 106

Voon Wong Architects
Unit 27
1 Stannary Street
London SW11 4AD, UK
Tel: +44 20 7587 0116
Fax: +44 20 7840 0178
email: Voon@dircon.co.uk
Page 68

José de Yturbe
De Yturbe Arquitectos
Patriotisimo 13 (4° piso)
Lomas de Barrilaco
Mexico 11010 DF
Tel: +525 540 368
Fax: +525 520 8621
Email: deyturbe infosel.net.mx
Pages 27, 59

Consuelo Zoelly
5–7 rue Mont Louis
75011 Paris, France
Tel: +33 1 42 62 19 95
Pages 88–89

credits

Key: a=above, b=below, l=left, r=right, c=center, ph=photographer

1 ph David Montgomery; **2** ph Andrew Wood/Alistair Hendy and John Clinch's apartment in London designed by Alistair Hendy; **2–3** ph David Brittain; 3al ph Ray Main/Lee F. Mindel's apartment in New York designed by Shelton, Mindel & Associates with Associate Architect Reed Morrison, lighting designed by Johnson Schwinghammer; 3br ph James Morris/Skywood House near London designed by Graham Phillips; **4** ph David Montgomery; **5** ph Polly Wreford; **7** ph David Brittain; **8** ph Polly Wreford/Clare Nash's house in London; **8–9** ph Andrew Wood/Alistair Hendy and John Clinch's apartment in London designed by Alistair Hendy; **10–11** ph Simon Upton; **12–13** ph Simon Upton/Barefoot Elegance; **14**al ph James Merrell; **14**br ph Andrew Wood/a house in London designed by Guy Stansfeld (+44 20 7727 0133); **15** ph Ray Main/Robert Callender and Elizabeth Ogilvie's studio in Fife designed by John C.Hope Architects; **16** ph Tom Leighton/Roger and Fay Oates' house in Herefordshire, The Long Barn, Eastnor, Ledbury, Herefordshire HR8 1EL, UK (+44 1531 632718); **17** ph Ray Main/Mark Jennings' apartment in New York designed by Asfour Guzy; **18** ph Simon Upton; **18–19** ph Henry Bourne; **20** ph Polly Wreford/Lena Proudlock's house in Gloucestershire; **21**l&r ph Polly Wreford; **22** ph Ray Main/light from Atrium; **23** ph Andrew Wood/Nicki de Metz's flat in London designed by de Metz Architects; **24** ph Ray Main/client's residence, East Hampton, NY, designed by ZG Design; **25** ph Ray Main/Jonathan Leitersdorf's apartment in New York designed by Jonathan Leitersdorf/Just Design Ltd; **26** ph Tom Leighton/Siobhan Squire and Gavin Lyndsey's loft in London designed by Will White, 326 Portobello Road, London W10 5RU, UK (+44 20 8964 8052); **27** ph Simon Upton; **28** ph Alan Williams/Gail and Barry Stephen's house in London; **29**al ph Ray Main/Lee F. Mindel's apartment in New York designed by Shelton, Mindel & Associates with Associate Architect Reed Morrison, lighting designed by Johnson Schwinghammer; **29**bl ph Ray Main/Jonathan Reed's apartment in London, lighting designed by Sally Storey, Design Director of John Cullen Lighting; **29**r Alan Williams/Andrew Wallace's house in London; **30** ph Simon Upton/Barefoot Elegance; **31** ph Simon Upton; **32** ph Andrew Wood/Heidi Kingstone's apartment in London; **32–33** ph David Brittain; **33**r ph Simon Upton/Barefoot Elegance; **34**l ph Catherine Gratwicke/Karen Harrison's house in London, cushions from Mint; **34**r ph Catherine Gratwicke/Intérieurs in New York; **35** ph Polly Wreford/Adria Ellis' apartment in New York, painting by Peter Zangrillo; **36** ph Henry Bourne; **37** ph Alan Williams/Katie Bassford King's house in London designed by Touch Interior Design; **38**al ph James Merrell; **38**bl ph Andrew Wood; **38**r ph Simon Upton/Barefoot Elegance; **39**l ph James Merrell; **39**r ph Polly Wreford/Ann Shore's house in London; **40**a ph Polly Wreford/Adria Ellis' apartment in New York; **40**b ph David Brittain; **41** ph Simon Upton; **42**l ph David Brittain; **42**r ph Catherine Gratwicke/Kimball Mayer and Megan Hughes' apartment in New York, designed by L.A. Morgan; **43** ph Simon Upton/Barefoot Elegance; **44** ph David Brittain; **44–45** ph James Merrell; **45**a ph Chris Everard; **45**b ph David Brittain; **46–47** all ph David Brittain; **48** ph James Merrell; **49** ph Polly Wreford/Ann Shore's house in London; **50**l ph Ray Main; **50**r, **50–51** ph Simon Upton; **52** ph Tom Leighton; **53**l ph Ray Main/Jamie Falla's house in London designed by MooArc; **53**r ph Tom Leighton/ceramic jars Carden Cunietti; **54**a ph Chris Everard; **54**b ph Alan Williams/Ms Feldman's house in New York by Patricia Seidman of Mullman Seidman Architects; **55** ph Alan Williams/Warner Johnson's apartment in New York designed by Edward Cabot at Cabot Design Ltd; **56**, **57**l&c ph James Merrell, **57**r ph Andrew Wood/Heidi Kingstone's apartment in London; **58**l ph Henry Bourne/Linda Trahair's house in Bath; **58**c&r ph Andrew Wood/Roger and Fay Oates' house in Herefordshire, The Long Barn, Eastnor, Ledbury, Herefordshire HR8 1EL, UK (+44 1531 632718); **59** ph Simon Upton; **60** ph Andrew Wood/Alistair Hendy and John Clinch's apartment in London designed by Alistair Hendy; **61** ph Andrew Wood/Han Feng's apartment in New York designed by Han Feng; **62 & 63**l ph Andrew Wood/Bernie de Le Cuona's house in Windsor: **63**r ph David Brittain: **64**l ph Andrew Wood/Mary Shaw's Sequana Apartment in Paris; **64**ar ph Tom Leighton; 64br ph Tom Leighton/Farrow & Ball colors; **65** ph Polly Wreford/Ann Shore's house in London; **66** ph Andrew Wood; **67**al ph Caroline Arber/Linda Garman's home in London; **67**bl ph Caroline Arber/Mary MacCarthy's house in Norfolk; **67**br ph Polly Wreford; **68** ph Alan Williams/the Architect Voon Wong's own apartment in London; **68–69** ph Polly Wreford/Marie-Hélène de Taillac's pied-à-terre in Paris; **70–71** ph Ray Main/Marina and Peter Hill's barn in West Sussex designed by Marina Hill, Peter James Construction Management, Chichester, The West Sussex Antique Timber Company, Wisborough Green, and Joanna Jefferson Architects; **72–73** all ph Tom Leighton; **74**l&r ph James Merrell; **75** ph Ray Main/Lee F. Mindel's apartment in New York designed by Shelton, Mindel & Associates with Associate Architect Reed Morrison, lighting designed by Johnson Schwinghammer; **76** ph Tom Leighton/Siobhan Squire and Gavin Lyndsey's loft in London designed by Will White, 326 Portobello Road, London W10 5RU, UK (+44 20 8964 8052); **77**l ph Polly Wreford/Carol Reid's apartment in Paris; **77**ar ph Chris Everard/Justin de Syllas and Annette Main's house in London, light courtesy of Artemide; **77**br ph Polly Wreford;

78l&r ph Andrew Wood/Guido Palau's house in North London designed by Azman Owens Architects; 79 ph James Merrell/an apartment in London designed by Ash Sakula Architects; 80 ph Simon Upton; 80–81 ph Andrew Wood/an apartment in Knokke, Belgium designed by Claire Bataille & Paul ibens; 82 ph Tom Leighton; 83al&br ph Simon Upton; 83ar & 84al ph Polly Wreford; 84br ph Caroline Arber; 85 ph David Montgomery; 86 ph James Merrell; 86–87 ph Simon Upton; 88al&bl ph James Merrell; 88–89 ph James Merrell/Consuelo Zoelly's apartment in Paris; 89 ph James Merrell/an apartment in London designed by Ash Sakula Architects; 90 ph James Merrell/Mike and Kris Taylor's loft in London designed by Circus Architects with Kayode Lipede; 91al&bl ph James Merrell; 91r & 92al ph David Loftus; 92bl ph David Brittain; 92r ph Andrew Wood/a house in London designed by Bowles & Linares; 93 ph James Merrell; 94 ph David Brittain; 95 ph Ray Main/Seth Stein's house in London; 96bl ph David Brittain; 96ar ph David Loftus; 97 ph Andrew Wood/Lims' House designed by Bedmar & Shi Designers in Singapore; 98–99 ph Ray Main/a house in London designed by Mark Guard Architects; 100a&b ph Tom Leighton/a loft in London designed by Robert Dye Associates; 101 ph James Merrell; 102–103 all ph Simon Upton; 104l ph Tom Leighton/Roger and Fay Oates' house in Herefordshire, The Long Barn, Eastnor, Ledbury, Herefordshire HR8 1EL, UK (+44 1531 632718); 104ar ph Polly Wreford/Kimberly Watson's house in London; 104br ph Polly Wreford/Ros Fairman's house in London; 105 ph Polly Wreford/Carol Reid's apartment in Paris; 106 ph Alan Williams/an apartment for Richard Oyarzarbal, by Urban Research Laboratory, London; 107a ph Andrew Wood/Heidi Kingstone's apartment in London; 107bl ph Ray Main/Kirk and Caroline Pickering's house in London, space creation by Square Foot Properties Ltd; 107br ph Henry Bourne; 108l&r ph Alan Williams/Alannah Weston's house in London designed by Stickland Coombe Architecture; 109l ph Ray Main/a loft in London designed by Nico Rensch, light from SKK; 109r ph James Merrell; 110–111 ph Chris Everard/a house in Hampstead, London designed by Orefelt Associates; 112l ph Andrew Wood/a house in London designed by Guy Stansfeld (+44 20 7727 0133); 112r ph Polly Wreford/Kathy Moskal's apartment in New York designed by Ken Foreman; 113 ph Chris Everard/a house in Surrey refurbished by Damien D'Arcy Associates; 114 & 115l ph Chris Everard/Sugarman-Behun house on Long Island; 115 ph David Montgomery; 116l ph Andrew Wood/a house at Jalan Berjaya, Singapore designed by Chan Soo Khian of SCDA Architects; 116r ph Chris Everard; 117 ph Chris Everard/a house in Paris designed by Bruno Tanquerel; 118–119 ph Andrew Wood/a house near Antwerp designed by Claire Bataille & Paul ibens; 119a ph Chris Everard/Simon Brignall and Christina Rosetti's loft in London designed by David Mikhail; 119b ph Andrew Wood/a house near Antwerp designed by Claire Bataille & Paul ibens; 120 ph Alan Williams/Alannah Weston's house in London designed by Stickland Coombe

Architecture; 121al&ar ph Chris Everard/Hilton McConnico's (interior house designer) house near Paris; 121b ph Henry Bourne/Dan & Claire Thorne's town house in Dorset designed by Sarah Featherstone; 122–123 ph Polly Wreford; 124l ph Polly Wreford/Marie-Hélène de Taillac's pied-à-terre in Paris; 124r ph Ray Main/light: Tizio by Richard Sapper, manufacturer: Artemide; 125l&r ph Andrew Wood/Babylon Design Ltd, studio in London; 126 ph Polly Wreford/an apartment in New York designed by Belmont Freeman Architects; 127al ph Ray Main/Thierry Watorek's house near Paris; 127bl ph Ray Main/Light by Tsé Tsé Associées, Catherine Levy and Sigolene Prebois; 127r ph Ray Main/light: Babylon Design Ltd; 128a ph Henry Bourne; 128bl ph Polly Wreford/Ann Shore's house in London; 128br ph Caroline Arber/Linda Garman's home in London; 129 ph Andrew Wood; 130–131 ph James Morris/Skywood House near London designed by Graham Phillips; 132a ph Jan Baldwin/Robert and Gabrielle Reeves' house in Clareville designed by Stutchbury & Pape Architects; 132b ph Andrew Wood/Johanne Riss' house in Brussels; 133 ph Ray Main/client's residence, East Hampton, NY, designed by ZG Design; 134 ph Jan Baldwin/Terry and Heather Dorrough's house on Dangar Island, NSW, designed by Terry Dorrough Architect; 135l ph Polly Wreford/Ann Shore's house in London; 135r ph James Merrell/a house in Pennsylvania designed by Laura Bohn and built by Richard Fiore/BFI Construction; 136a ph Andrew Wood/Lims' House designed by Bedmar & Shi Designers in Singapore; 136b ph Simon Upton; 137 ph Jan Baldwin/Les Reedman's house on Dangar Island, NSW; 144 ph David Brittain; endpapers ph David Brittain.

In addition to the homeowners mentioned, we would also like to thank the following people: Clare Mannix-Andrews, Mr and Mrs Ruttenberg, Conner Prarie Museum, Dot Spikings, Sherri Donghia and Robert Eulau, Tricia Foley, José Yturbe, Jo Saker, James Lynch and Sian Tucker, Frank and Suz Cameron, Katsuji Asada, Jim Ruscitto, Ricardo Regazzoni, Guido Stockman, Potted Gardens, Claire Farrow and William Morris, Jane Cumberbatch, Frazer Cunningham, Atlanta Bartlett, and Elie Mouyal.

index

acknowledgments

Thank you to Sophie, Alison, Sally, Jenny, and Emily, who have worked
so hard to produce this book.